D0442983

COMMANDER OF THE *EXODUS*

BOOKS BY YORAM KANIUK
PUBLISHED BY GROVE PRESS

Commander of the Exodus
Adam Resurrected

Commander of the *Exodus*

By Yoram Kaniuk
Translated by
Seymour Simckes

Grove Press
New York

First published in the Hebrew language by Hakibbutz Hameuchad Publishing
House and Daniela Di-Nur.

Published by arrangement with the Institute for the Translation of Hebrew
Literature.

Published simultaneously in Canada
Printed in the United States of America

FIRST EDITION

Library of Congress Cataloging-in-Publication Data

Kaniuk, Yoram.
    [Eksodus. English]
    Commander of the Exodus/by Yoram Kaniuk ; translated by Seymour
Simckes.
        p. cm.
    ISBN 0-8021-1664-7
    1. Exodus 1947 (Ship) 2. Harel, Yossi. 3. Palestine—Emigration and
immigration. 4. Refugees, Jewish—Palestine. 5. Holocaust survivors—
Palestine. 6. Jews—Palestine—History—20th century. I. Simckes,
Seymour. II. Title.

DS126.4.K237 2000
305.892405694—dc21   00-022898

Design by Laura Hammond Hough

Grove Press
841 Broadway
New York, NY 10003

00 01 02 03 10 9 8 7 6 5 4 3 2 1

Long live the lads who got the command
And sailed by the line through the fogs
On target, on time, though hunted like dogs
With no map and no compass in hand.

Their tale too will get told, that's for sure
For the waves and the skies they observed
On a single, near-sinking ship unswerved
How they fought so the nation might endure.

—Nathan Alterman,
"A Sermon in Response to an Italian Captain
after a Night of Disembarking"

Author's Note

first met Yossi Harel many years after he led the legendary expeditions that brought Jews to Palestine in the 1940s and years after he had been engaged in some of Israel's most secret affairs—missions that make James Bond's exploits seem like child's play. He and a friend had opened a large swimming pool in Tel Aviv, and it was then that I became acquainted with him. He did not seem to me the kind of man who could have done the things I knew he had done—that is, the little I knew of his feats, anyway. To this day Yossi does not readily disclose his stories. Ask him why, and he'll declare, "Because!" That is his way. When he goes to Jerusalem he will tell me he is going to Haifa; he still does not trust speech, because the enemy—whatever, or whoever, that may be—might be listening.

We talked a good deal then, but became friends only years later. I was interested in the people he had brought over from Europe in the 1940s—most of them survivors of the Holocaust—and I knew that he was one of the only ones to embrace them then. At that time many Israelis were concerned chiefly with the drama that was unfolding on their own territory: the incessant Arab revolts, the constant tensions wrought by the British Mandate, the urgent need to establish an official state. The plight of the European Jews was not necessarily at the top of their agenda. Yossi understood intuitively that these survivors (whom many Palestine Jews scornfully called "soaps," which was what their less fortunate brothers, the ones killed in the gas chambers, were made into by the Nazis) constituted the very reason they were fighting for a state to begin with. For Yossi, bringing the refugees to Palestine upstaged all other concerns.

I decided to document Yossi's story. He sat with me for months and, though he talked, clearly withheld much, keeping the soul of his tale unremittingly dry and phlegmatic. Eventually I threatened to quit, and when he continued to resist I did just that. A few years later, however, his son called me and said that he knew how many years I had been sitting with Yossi, learning nothing and wanting to write, and he said, "My father is going to be eighty years old. Perhaps I can convince him to cooperate." And so he did.

We talked for days, and again he resisted, withheld, and tried to divert me; soon it became clear that his fierce privacy owed much to the fact that he had sealed his voice in tribute to his many friends who had died along the way and were buried along with their secrets. When I finally convinced him that he could trust me to interpret his words myself, without using his voice, his remarkable story slowly emerged. Here was a man who had never learned Kant's moral categories, yet the stones of barren Jerusalem, his adventurous soul, and his stalwart sense of responsibility combined to create what no university can teach. And so this book is meant to fill the space of his known and defiant silence.

The publication of this book in Israel coincided with Yossi's eightieth birthday, and his family threw a gala affair in celebration. It was a momentous and moving event, and President Ezer Weizmann came and told wonderful stories about this man of iron and soul, a man impelled by equal measures of toughness and hidden softness. The guests talked, sang, ate, and had their copies of the book signed by the man who changed the course of their nation's history. He knew he was giving himself away, but he also knew that he was doing it with grace. I was the stool pigeon who had betrayed him. Writers should be betrayers; he asserted that too happily. So Yossi can defend himself by smiling that mysterious smile of one who has worked me over and won. In truth, both of us are the winners, or the losers. He knows that, too.

Prologue

The State of Israel was not established on May 15, 1948, when the official declaration was made at Tel Aviv Museum. It was born nearly a year earlier on July 18, 1947, when a battered and stricken American ship called *President Warfield*, whose name was changed to *Exodus*, entered the port of Haifa with its loudspeakers blaring the strains of "Hatikva."

The State of Israel came into existence before it acquired a name, when its gates were locked to Jews, when the British fought against survivors of the Holocaust. It came into existence when its shores were blockaded—against those for whom the state was eventually designated—by forty-five model C warships, the most modern warships the British built toward the end of World War II, which hadn't managed to see service. The fleet was gigantic even by today's standards: cruisers, destroyers, mine sweepers, state-of-the-art patrol boats of the Sinbad 2 variety that were armored and fast, plus a division of the Royal Air Force consisting of planes from Palestine, Cyprus, Egypt, and Malta. It came into being when they closed its gates by means of tens of thousands of soldiers, thousands of police and intelligence agents from the CID, on land, in the ports, and throughout Europe, and by means of detention camps in Atlit and Cyprus.

Israel came into being on the day that His Royal Majesty's sailors attacked the passengers of a ship recently taken from the Potomac River on the eastern seaboard of the United States, where it had concluded its long life as an obsolete ferryboat slated for salvage. The British lobbed hundreds of tear gas grenades on those trapped inside, 4,515 human beings who two years previously had been rescued from another gas, in another place.

As the ship was towed slowly into Haifa Bay under the watchful eyes of the delegates of UNSCOP, the Anglo-American committee appointed by the UN to find a solution to the Palestine problem, Bartley Crum, the famous attorney and member of UNSCOP, likened the incident to the Boston Tea Party. Out of this encounter between *Exodus* and the delegates brought to Haifa after the report of the ship's arrival, out of the expertise of the ship's commanders, and especially out of the torment of its passengers, their frustration after being attacked at sea along the coast of Palestine, and their despair during the agonizing journey of deportation to Germany, where they were thrown into Camp Poppendorf not far from Hamburg, a former Nazi concentration camp—out of all this the Jewish state was born before it was established.

People were crammed like sardines on the ancient deck, with living quarters 50 centimeters wide, 1.8 meters long, and 90 centimeters high between bunks. They came because they had nowhere else to go. Most of the survivors claimed that they wanted to live in a land of their own, in a house of their own, but even if they did not want it, they had no other choice since the possibility of immigrating to America, Britain, Canada, Australia, Latin America, and Belgium was limited. Between the years 1945 and 1948 all these countries together had granted only twenty-five thousand Jewish Holocaust survivors entry into their borders.

Thus, a young girl as anxious as an alley cat, barely sixteen years old, her dark eyes in a dull daze, a girl the Germans had turned into a camp whore for the SS and on whose chest had tattooed *Feldhure A. 13652,* sang on the bridge of the *Knesset Israel* a song taught to her by Yossi Harel, the ship's commander. This lost yet courageous girl sat on the bridge, held an old guitar in her hands, stared into the eyes of the British boarding the ship, and in sorrow, in calm contempt, sang the song by Alterman,

"Sleep Deep, Glorious Land"; this girl overcame the British with a song about a landscape she never knew, in a language she did not understand.

The arrival of *Exodus* from Europe was a unique historical encounter between the Jewish community in Palestine, known as the *yishuv*, which had developed its own mentality, and Jewish suffering in the Diaspora. After 1933, from the time Hitler rose to power until the British practically halted immigration in 1939, permitting only seventy-five thousand Jews to immigrate in the ensuing five years, the Jewish population of Palestine counted an increasing number of new immigrants to the land. Legal immigration, though, was denied the majority of those wanting to come. The only remaining option was illegal immigration.

From 1934 to 1948, 115,000 Jews either reached Palestine or were caught by the British. The *Dalin*, the first ship brought by Mossad le-Aliyah Beth, the Organization for Illegal Immigration, at the close of the war in August 1945 carried thirty-five refugees to the shores of Caesaria. The two *Pans*, *Pan York* and *Pan Crescent*, the ships Yossi Harel sailed in 1948 that basically concluded the chapter of illegal immigration during the British Mandate (about six small ships arrived thereafter), brought 15,236 people.

Between the end of the thirties and the beginning of the forties—despite the myths, songs, and praises heaped upon this period of illegal immigration—few refugees landed on the shores of Palestine. Most of the attempts failed. The British detained the refugees in camps in Atlit and later in Cyprus, but even while they were in the Cypriot camps they were already on their way to the land of Israel. That is, they had already left Europe. Resettling was no small matter. The actions of the Haganah also helped. But Jewish terrorist tactics, as courageous as they were, managed merely to harass a superb army that knew how to crush major uprisings in various lands, an army that survived Dunkirk. Such tactics only irritated and vexed soldiers of a nation that persisted bravely during the Blitz. What vanquished the British empire in Palestine was the scrutiny of the destitute girl, that camp whore of the SS, her intense rage, the fearless way she sat on the bridge and sang, in the midst of the heavy attack, what sounded like a grim lullaby while the British stormed the almost sinking ship. What broke the British was their helplessness in the face of thousands of people who continued to come without a stop, aboard ship after ship. In order to reach the shores of Palestine they crawled up mountain paths of Europe, trekked through snow-covered forests, waited in detention camps under subhuman conditions, froze in the cold, starved, and kept coming.

Some portions of this book blend historical truth with imagination. I don't pretend that all the details are incontestable. But no detail, alone or in combination, can alter the total picture or full impact and historical significance of these events. This is the saga of Yossi Harel and the exodus from Europe. It is not a traditional biography, but it is absolutely based on the facts.

Many good people participated in the rescue effort: dozens of Mossad le-Aliyah Beth agents and seventy to eighty Palmach members active on the boats and in the camps. I chose to tell the story from the point of view of a single individual, a young man who commanded four ships in the mid-1940s—the largest ones in the saga of illegal immigration—compelled by his own moral responsibility and an audacity bordering on adventurism, in which thousands of people who had abandoned everything were crammed in the depths of rickety tubs, with barely a life raft or two available, without life belts. And he was just twenty-seven.

When these starving, beaten people sang "Hatikva" on the deck of the *Exodus*, Yossi imagined that the victims of the Inquisition must have sung likewise. The sight of the refugees huddled over their baggage, hugging their belongings, clarified for him that he, no less than the British with all their chicanery, was obligated to succeed. Britain had indeed won the war, but utterly lost the peace. After World War II a severe food shortage prevailed in Britain. In the cities—London included—people stood in line for food and clothing distributed in exchange for ration coupons. The British did not have enough funds to return thousands of their soldiers from Greece. In Haifa, after the British took control of *Exodus* and removed the refugees, the sailors of His Royal Majesty found tin cans of kosher meat shipped from America by the Joint Distribution Committee. The British fumed: England suffers a grave food shortage while luck shines on these obstinate Jews! They appropriated the tins of kosher meat and shipped them to their families in Britain.

Yet simultaneously the British government managed to disburse a fortune in order to maintain in Palestine tens of thousands of soldiers to prevent an invasion of Holocaust survivors they themselves had helped rescue two years earlier.

In order to seize ships in extraterritorial waters far offshore, the British dredged up—from the bottom of cynicism's barrel—a seventeenth-century slave trade statute that allowed this practice. After all, it is permissible to circumvent the law now and again, they said, and who says navigation is an exact science! In fact, Yossi Harel, like the other blockade-running commanders, also practiced this inexact activity. His secret lay in the insight he gained about the Diaspora Jew he was taught in his youth to look down on. This Palestine-born young man, schooled by the struggle against Arab terrorist bands in the hills of Jerusalem or Hanita, learned to understand and love the frail women aboard the ships, the ashen-faced men, frightened, angry, nightmare ridden, who wore their clothing in three or four layers.

Yossi, known to many by his underground name "Amnon," wanted to be their guide rather than their overseer. He honored their misery as both the fruit of years of wandering and the measure of their courage, something few other than they themselves understood in those days. Yossi would never forget how at the height of a storm, as waves swept across the decks past the midpoint of the masts, women and young girls burst onto the frigid deck when it was their turn for duty, stripped naked, and bathed themselves in the cold water to preserve their human image. He understood the shame and disgrace, the force and fury, they carried in them. He understood the strength of their survival instinct in the face of such an enormous betrayal, when all the doors of the world were shut against them, and he felt he had to support and uphold them with his very own hands. They were, in his words, lighted blue candles, a precious bequest entrusted to him.

A sense of partnership evolved. To transport hundreds of thousands of people from German transit camps through an armed British blockade, one had to have unequivocal convictions. It was always all or nothing; hardly some academic deliberation on whether historical justice could be viewed as human or po- litical injustice.

When he commanded the *Knesset Israel* a few months be- fore he sailed the *Exodus*, Yossi met a lad of eighteen who saved himself at age thirteen by pretending he was dead. The boy wan- dered from place to place, joined the Red Army, blew the bugle, and reached as far as Siberia and back again to the Baltic front. At the end of the war he returned as a Romanian patriot to his home in Bucharest with a sack of old clothes and a bugle. None of his neighbors wanted him around. He was removed from his parents' home, which was confiscated by strangers. His parents had vanished, and he did not know their fate. He reached the ship embracing his sole possession on earth, his bugle. When Yossi saw how tightly he held it, as if it were his solitary family heir- loom, Yossi befriended him in compassion and respect and gave him an armband emblazoned with the symbol of a bugle, and whenever he had to make an announcement, the boy would go to some designated spot and sound the trumpet. Yossi's ability, or perhaps necessity, to understand the boy was truly personal, yet it was based as well on the precepts of Mossad le-Aliyah Beth, the organization to which he belonged, whose members called it the "Aristocratic Service." These agents worked alone, each in- dividual on his own—in cities, in ports, in far-flung mountain passes. This approach grew from how they contacted survivors without any intermediary. One of them said, "I saw famished Romanian Jews in tattered worn-out clothes rushing across the borders. They were indifferent to bullets or arrest." And Yossi said, "We in Palestine always had a home to return to, family, friends. But to be so cut off . . ."

While sailing at sea on the *Knesset Israel*, one day Yossi noticed that the coal-run steamship was slowing down. Below, in the engine room, the temperature had reached fifty to sixty degrees centigrade. On the deck the orchestra was rehearsing in a rainstorm for a party scheduled that evening. In one of the sweltering storerooms, a woman named Esther M. was conducting the rehearsal of a play to be staged that night.

Yossi went to see what was blocking the coal loading process. Beside a life raft, one of the few on the ship, he found some of the engineers taking a short break. Dark brown from soot, they had come up to escape the blazing heat of the engine room. They hung together like a statue of multiple figures in one cast, head resting on head, hands locked on each other's shoulders. They were so attached to each other, so entangled, you could not tell which head belonged to the hand that dropped or which hand belonged to the head that suddenly nodded. The statue froze on the spot, all its eyes focused on the sea. Yossi felt, in the tense silence, a strain of fear derived from elsewhere, an old terror of another scene, like camouflaging oneself as a statue that does not move. Although their gaze was fixed on the sea, Yossi realized they really did not see it. The sea they saw was not in their eyes.

Not far from them stood a young man alone, as though chained to the deck, wrapped in solitude, locked inside it. He too had come up for air. He too stared at the sea and did not see it. His stance by the many-headed, many-handed statue appeared forsaken and fixed. He trembled. His tears froze in his eyes. His loneliness seemed a kind of stubbornness and, at the same time, an attempt to catch the elusive waves he could not actually see because of the tears rolling down his face. For a moment, at the sound of Yossi's footsteps, he turned his eyes, which looked empty. The solitary figure and the ensemble did not exchange glances but gave the impression that together—solo figure and statuesque cluster—they formed a unit, though a wall separated them.

In the middle of the multihanded statue, as if encased by a bubble, stood a nearly suffocating young woman, her pale face whitened in transparent pain, who looked like a faded photograph. She remained silent. Her silence, on the threshold of a scream, together with the utter muteness of the solitary young man opposite her, formed a difficult dialogue of sorts. Each of them in isolation peered at an abyss that was both shared and separate, and they remained silent.

Yossi could not unravel the import of this scene, and it bothered him. He inquired, investigated, and ultimately learned that in the concentration camp, when the young man was a boy of fourteen, he was ordered to receive the new transports. At the entrance there was a narrow passageway between two barbed-wire fences. At the far end the passage divided into two lanes, one to the work camp and the other to what he called, as he unfolded his story, the "ovens." At the intersection stood the German doctor who selected people with a wag of his finger. Suddenly the boy spotted a young woman carrying a child in her arms, hurrying on, while a woman who seemed to him to be her mother trudged behind. A few steps before the selection juncture, as the German averted his face for a moment, the boy snatched the child from the shocked mother and flung it into the arms of the old woman. The mother shrieked, but he ignored her. The doctor did not notice. He looked back and sent the young mother to the work camp. After several days the heartbroken young woman tried to kill herself, but the other women in her barracks prevented her. And here on the deck, in a stormy night, with a female orchestra playing in the background, Yossi Harel from Jerusalem witnessed the first meeting of the young man and the woman. The first meeting since he had grabbed her child from her. It was an encounter without anger. Without pardon. Without a glance. Without judgment.

COMMANDER OF THE *EXODUS*

Chapter One

When the persecutions of the Jews began to assume a fierce momentum in Europe, Yossi Harel was fighting in Jerusalem and the Galilee against Arabs in the anti-Jewish riots of the 1930s. The Palestinian conflict, too, was already a struggle for existence to determine who would survive.

Yossi was born in Jerusalem in 1919 to Moshe and Batya Hamburger, both of whose families had first come to Palestine in the nineteenth century. His childhood was not a simple one. His father ran a grocery and looked after his children and his wife, who was a lovely, aristocratic woman, but also extremely fragile emotionally. She was eccentric, withdrawn, and quite troubled, and at that time they did not know how to treat her.

Perhaps in a subconscious attempt to compensate for his mother's fragility, Yossi was a solid block of decisions, measured feelings, and objective facts; he shaped his character consciously and deliberately. He loved his mother as every son does, but in her madness he felt betrayal. When it became too difficult to live with the guilt that took hold of him in her presence, Yossi instinctively recognized the only way to protect himself: he decided his mother was dead. He separated himself from her while she was still living and did not see her again until she died many years later.

Because of all the damage wrought by his troubled childhood and the sense of betrayal bound up in his relationship with his mother, Yossi was later able to identify with the pain of the orphans he brought by ship to Palestine for these very reasons.

Those children were in some ways a reflection of himself. They were also his atonement.

When he completed the statutory requirements of his public education at Tachkemoni School, Yossi got a job working in the Castel quarries to help out his family, and soon thereafter he also worked for the post office in Jerusalem, laying underground telephone wires. At age fourteen he enlisted in the Haganah, the Jewish army, along with his friends from the Boy Scout Legion; in one way or another he stayed within this framework until he became a man of forty.

While his close friends studied at high school, Yossi continued to work and was forced to prepare for the external exams of the London Matriculation. At age eighteen, when he was still active in the Haganah, his father, sister, and twin brother went down to Sodom to run a cafeteria for the Dead Sea project, a community undertaking initiated by the workers movement. Yossi remained alone. His circle of friends in the movement and in the Haganah replaced his family, even while he kept supporting his mother, whom he no longer saw.

One of his strongest memories—one that later grieved him and served as a milestone in his Haganah ventures—was connected to the riots of 1929. At age eleven he went with the Boy Scout Legion to a workers camp in Kibbutz Kiryat Anavim, near Jerusalem. Two days later, early Saturday morning, the campers were notified they were being disbanded and returned to Jerusalem. Loaded onto a truck, they were driven home with an armored escort. En route they passed by Castel and its foothills along a twisting road with seven curves known as the Seven Sisters and reached the village of Motsa.

This small Jewish settlement, situated within a large Arab region, had been attacked and destroyed in the night. It was still ablaze as they approached. The rioters had butchered six people, among them all the children of the Maklef family, except for the boy Mordechai (who would later go on to be the Israel Defense Force's third chief of staff). Blankets soaked in blood covered the dissected body parts. When he reached Jerusalem with his friends, Yossi joined the throngs of Jews streaming from all parts of the city with sticks in their hands. In Zichron Moshe, opposite the Edison Cinema, there was a huge gathering. A furious crowd demanded revenge. Among them were Russian Jews from Georgia, wielding ancient swords they still kept in their homes. Bit by bit the news trickled in about the riots in Hebron and Safed. At that time, in those hours, the boy formulated a lifelong manifesto. With a profound earnestness only the very young are capable of, he resolved that the slaughter of Jews for simply being Jews must never happen in this land. It was up to him, a man of eleven, to struggle to prevent a repetition of such acts. The scenes in Motsa, the dismembered corpses covered in sheets, the smoldering houses—these Yossi would remember for the rest of his life.

Yossi and his friends formed very strong bonds, their "togetherness" a substitute for family. Mature but romantic youths, they trained in utter seriousness, which was sometimes exaggerated, overzealous, and steeped in high-blown clichés, in order to become heroes under the influence of the ideology they absorbed in youth movements and at school. They stuck to one another, a captive band from small adjoining neighborhoods of Jerusalem, the most Jewish city in the landscape of the Zionist rebirth. They prepared themselves to be fighters, they debated ideology with an intensity bordering on fanaticism, and at the same time they played Jewish musketeers. They lived in a little town veiled in the dust of former glory, the glory of a grand city long since faded and reduced to poverty, shrunk to a smattering of minuscule neighborhoods and a multitude of stones. Save for the Old City and several old neighborhoods, the scorched landscape, exposed to the sun, was planted mainly with stones and lined with wide-branched olive trees. Unlike the sands of Tel Aviv, Jerusalem, with its endless gray stone, rocks, snakes, and empty lots gathered like flocks of lost sheep among magnificent but isolated and secluded structures—mosques, churches, holy places—was all of a piece. Stone, rock, and tree filled a topography turned occult.

When they climbed Mt. Scopus to train and prepare for battle, they considered themselves biblical heroes. They looked around and saw how the inhabited Western world ended where they stood and the desert began. All their lives they had lived physically and spiritually on the edge of the desert's wasteland, on the verge of the mysterious, the terrifying. They had dreams of conquering the world.

When he was fourteen Yossi decided to head out for Masada by himself. Jews had concealed that story of courage and suicide for two thousand years. It appeared in just one Jewish book, *The Jewish War*, by Joseph ben Matityahu, aka Josephus Flavius, the commander of Fortress Gamla, a genius considered a traitor. After he surrendered in order to save his men, he joined the Romans. At the start of clashes with the Arabs in 1920, the fanatical nationalistic dimension was absent, despite the atrocities, but then the saga of Masada was reborn because, after all, a war requires a myth. This was a dark and menacing myth, intoxicating in its simplicity, soaked in dread. The nation needed heroes, and heroes needed a past to latch on to. Courage and sacrifice transposed into moral imperatives rather than mere strategies for survival. The heroes who served that purpose were the heroes of the Bible and the heroes of the revolt against the Romans. In the face of poverty and despair, the educational system offered prepackaged ideas. Masada seemed like a suitable heroic chapter for those born in the land and for Jews come from the ghettos of Eastern Europe. The youth in Palestine had much to overcome, much to reclaim. Intense focus was essential, even if it would later appear horrific and savage: the sanctification of heroic death, of the collective suicide Jews tried to suppress and expunge from all their books.

It took Yossi three long days to cross the desert. At that time it was extremely perilous to cross the desert alone, on account of predatory beasts and Arab rioters. But a sense of "national mission," as it was called in those days, presented itself before his eyes as he made the treacherous ascent to Masada. He stood on the mountain facing the Dead Sea and felt close to the rebels and proud of the spiritual strength he found in himself to make it here on his own, evading snakes, Bedouins, and the heat and knowing that despite the dangers he was unafraid.

Yossi returned from his trek ecstatic and exhausted. Traversing the desert, he attained the desideratum of revenge, annihilation, adventure, and zealotry. Through this trip, and others that he took, mostly alone, he taught himself to be a man of the field, thus laying the foundation for the rules of self-reliance that would serve him all his life. He taught himself not to depend on backup; to know that if something went wrong and you cried out, nobody would hear you; to know how to stand up straight but to recognize that if there was a sudden shift in the desert wind, it was an act of bravery to bend. Yossi and his friends cultivated the image of the fighting Israeli. But the secular Palestinian Yossi from the Boy Scout Legion was also the son of Jerusalem, which was religious, non-Zionist, even partially anti-Zionist for the segment that lived in Palestine as though it were still in the Diaspora. He came from a small grocery store that served as a chess club at night, from a grandfather who was a fourth-generation Jerusalemite and built a synagogue, from a traditional Jerusalem home. Although Yossi grew up in a landscape of sentimental sunsets, of song and declamation in youth-movement gatherings on kibbutz lawns, he was also present at synagogues and cemeteries of the Old City in the Mount of Olives, where notables were buried as close as possible to the Temple Mount in order to be the first ones to greet the Messiah.

As very young men, Yossi and his friends read *The Forty Days of Musa Dagh*, a book by Franz Werfel about the Armenian revolt in the mountains of Anatolia. They found in this book a moral code. Hidden within it, the book contained pain and bravery, loyalty and isolation, and it won the hearts of the young Palestine Jews.

Years later, on the nearly empty deck of a ship teeming with refugees and under a full moon, it would all come together—Masada, Musa Dagh, the lessons of Yossi's youth. As the ship sailed in blood-curdling quiet along the Turkish coast, what preoccupied Yossi on this junkheap ready to capsize was his compulsive probe through binoculars, maps, intuition and childhood memories, in search of Mt. Musa Dagh. It was winter, the ship was packed with almost 4,500 people, but Yossi—like an ultra-Orthodox Jew clutching the Wailing Wall—held onto the mountain. He was Musa Dagh on the deck, approaching the mountain where the American survivors of genocide entrenched themselves and fought. Finally, he spotted it in the distance, capped in snow, and it called to mind his trip to Masada. He thought about the barrenness of the arid mountain, and how several years earlier he had stood at its foot and inspected the parched landscape, the most desolate landscape in the world, the desert that resembled the face of the moon, and felt in his bones and all his veins the anguish of those beseiged on Masada, who for nine months watched the Romans build, bit by bit, the embankments that signaled their deaths to come. Their eyes perceived the inevitable, but they could no longer flee, so they committed suicide—in the biting brilliance spraying from the Dead Sea at the foot of the mountain.

Chapter Two

Yitzhak Sadeh, the legendary revolutionary hero who perhaps more than anyone else influenced the establishment of Jewish power in Palestine, was Yossi's first spiritual and military father. Sir Isaiah Berlin, Sadeh's first cousin, was accustomed to calling him "the Jewish Garibaldi" and wrote that he was "the bravest, most cheerful, charming, enriching man I ever knew . . . one of the exceptions of life, superb in time of war and revolution, but dull in the course of tranquil, orderly, unstormy, day-to-day life." At the age of forty-six Sadeh arrived in Jerusalem to establish a fighting unit of a new kind.

This was just after Germany enacted the Nuremberg Laws in September 1935, after at least one German medical journal concluded that "the comparison of Jews with tubercular bacteria is accurate, for Jews are a chronic infection." The "Fifth Aliyah" was then at its height, with an organized uprooting of Jews from the German scene. Between 1935 and 1939 about 150,000 Jews fortunate enough to be granted papers came to Palestine from Germany, Holland, Austria, and Czechoslovakia. In these four years, the Jewish population in Palestine doubled itself. Of course this flow of legal immigration ended when the British issued the White Paper in 1939, which provided for severely low quotas of immigration visas in light of the ever growing number of Jews wanting to flee. In turn, the only Jews that set out for Palestine did so illegally, and a large number of them died in the process.

In these years, the Arabs did not approve of the stream of refugees coming into their quarters. There was a generalized feel-

7

ing among them of "If a house is on fire *there*, why must they leap into *our* courtyard?" So they launched what they called the Great Revolt, which became the first chapter in a sixty-year-old war between Arabs and Jews that still rages today.

Sadeh had certain ideas about how to deal with the conflict. He had been a yeshiva student as a boy, but later became a true revolutionary, an officer in the Russian Revolution; he left only because he could not stomach the rampant anti-Semitism. He came to Palestine to join the Haganah and to try to introduce innovative tactics, whereby soldiers would not be confined to the trenches but would actually infiltrate the side of the enemy. Such innovations did not appeal to the old guard, many of whom were veterans from the Great War, so Sadeh set about finding reliable men who were daring enough to share his vision and actually execute it.

He found the fighters he was looking for among Jerusalem's youth groups, in Yossi Harel and his friends. From the moment Sadeh arrived at their post, they were dazzled. Nobody had ever spoken to them with such fierceness, such intense sharp ideas. Such was the origin of the active unit that Sadeh, ever the romantic, dubbed the Nomads. In time it would prove to be the mother and father of the future reconnaissance units of the Israel Defense Force.

Sadeh led them on nightly raids he referred to as "putting out the lights in Arab villages." He maintained that it wasn't fair that Jews had to hide in their homes in the dark while Arabs sat in the light, taking pot shots at them. He taught them to ambush the rioters, to leave their pillboxes and trenches.

Yossi, known as "the Playboy of the Nomads" because of his tender age and pretty face; pensive Tsvi Spector, the unit's father figure and bibliophile; wild Abdu, the risk-taking fighter; and the quiet, wise Yitzchak Heker—all became Sadeh's men. The mission was to build a smart and bold concentrated unit to guard the settlements in the Jerusalem area. Sadeh said, "Instead of their coming to you, you go to them. Our forces are few. The night will magnify our numbers. The Arab knows the terrain. His tracking skill is superior to ours. He knows how to slip away, how to hide, he's a good soldier. Our strength lies in the element of surprise, stealth, and the darkness of night."

In his eyes, Palestine-born Jews were the wonders of Jewish history, embodiments of biblical heroes without the Diaspora humpback. He himself was heavyset and rough. His vision was poor. From a kilometer away they could hear him trudging. Sometimes he came across like a poet that showed up by mistake. But for them he was a commander in the full sense of the word. "When you're small," he repeated, "be nimble, brilliant, full of tricks, and above all, audacious."

Sadeh slept naked, exercised alone in the morning, then bathed in cold water. He was accustomed to talking about tactics and feats of bravery for hours, weaving poems and philosophy into his lesson and the fruits of his experience as a fighter in the Russian Revolution and thereafter in Palestine. He also knew when to keep silent as a stone; he was lovable and open, yet also self-absorbed and cryptic. Under his command the Nomads used sudden loud bursts of gunfire in open terrain as a tactic to get the enemy to overestimate their strength in numbers and firepower. His philosophy was, *Whatever works for the enemy can work for you, too.* "A small nation," he contended, "in a small land like ours, doesn't get a second chance. The nation has nowhere to hide, beyond what the poet Alterman called 'the trenches of life.'" Sadeh taught Yossi and his friends to believe they were truly serving the nation, but they would get nothing in return. There was no budget, no state to finance them.

Abdu, Tsvi Spector, and Yossi heard of a massacre of Jews in the Old City, the killing of a guard near Givat Shaul, the attempt to set fire to a nursery in the Baka neighborhood, and the killing of three Jews in downtown Jerusalem in Edison Square. They didn't tell a soul of their plan. Intent on revenge, they armed themselves and headed for the Jaffa gate to hit the members of a gang they assumed they would find there. When they saw that British soldiers were patrolling the area, they retreated and altered their plan. They took off for Abu-Gosh, where they hurled some grenades into a coffeehouse. A handful of Arabs were sitting inside. The grenades caused a ruckus, but no one was killed. Afterward, they shot indiscriminately at some harvesters in a field in Colonia, the village out of which came the killers at Motsa. Although they were actually brought to trial, the Haganah needed them, so they returned to serve under Yitzhak Sadeh, who closed more than one eye when he learned of this business. They discovered—perhaps from remorse as well as anger over their lack of success—that anger and vengeful feelings are the true Achilles' heels of good soldiers.

Yossi loved Sadeh, known as "the old man" even while still relatively young. He was a lonely man who gave his all but did not know how to make genuine contact with others. He was not fully disciplined as a soldier—daring, but unlike Yossi, he was sentimental, an adventurer who acted responsibly. Yossi admired him as an outstanding general able to grasp the whole picture, laying out perfect strategies, then leaving the plans to the commanders he chose. Although nobody could predict it at the time, Sadeh would go on to become one of the greatest Jewish generals of our day. To Yossi, who had already broken from his family and his past, Sadeh was a secular rebbe sought after by his disciples as though he had come from another world to transport them to a reality that had already taken shape in their romantic eyes.

In July 1937 the British Peel Commission issued its report. It investigated the explosive response of the Arabs to increased Jewish emigration from Germany, Austria, Czechoslovakia, and Poland. The Arabs hoped that the rise of the Fascists in Italy and the Nazis in Germany would strengthen them through a joint pact against the English and the Jews. The Peel Commission studied the stormy situation in Palestine and proposed that the country be partitioned into two entities, Arab and Jewish. In the Woodhead Commission's Report, which followed almost immediately on November 9, 1938, the Jewish area was cut in half. A new high commissioner arrived in Palestine, Sir Harold MacMichael, a colonial secretary hostile to the Jewish side. In contrast to his predecessor, Sir Arthur Wauchope, who opened the gates of Palestine to a limited though not negligible number of Jewish refugees, MacMichael faithfully advocated the pro-Arab hard line.

According to the Peel plan, the Galilee was to be included in the area under Jewish jurisdiction, but the new British Mandate administration did everything it could to tear off western Galilee and transfer it to Arab hands. For the Palestinian leaders, the Galilee became the critical issue. The song "God Will Build the Galilee" became a Jewish national anthem of sorts. Lush, large, distant, the Galilee constituted a crucial barrier against Syria and Lebanon. At that time the region was heavily attacked by hundreds of Arab agitators, some of whom came well trained and well armed from Lebanon and Syria. They fought with ferocious spirit. Their skill and great numbers made it difficult to come up with the proper counteraction. The Nomads were already disbanded, and in their place Sadeh had instituted field squads known as FOSH, comprising the boldest fighters he knew. In 1938, as Yossi was about to leave to fight in the Spanish civil war, Sadeh summoned him to inform him that they were preparing to go up to Hanita in Galilee, and it would be his task to serve as chief weapons instructor.

Palestine was riddled with funerals. Bloody disturbances had already lasted for two years. New immigrants who had just arrived fought and were buried under tombstones inscribed "Unknown" or "Anonymous." People began to show signs of despair. They wanted to retaliate, to strike the enemy that was no longer just a constellation of terrorist bands, but were regular soldiers, suddenly strong and very prepared.

At the news of the settlement in Hanita, the *yishuv* felt relief and enthusiasm. Planned over a period of more than two months, it was the largest military settlement project the Jews of Palestine had undertaken up to that point. Thousands wished to settle there. Only a few hundred were accepted. Girls born that year were named Hanita. Hanita became the Wild West of Palestine, right in the heart of a huge, hostile, densely populated Arab region fully armed and trained by the Iraqis and Syrians. In the eyes of the leadership of the Jewish community, Hanita was the natural geographic border of the land of Israel. The Arabs and their leaders were no fools. Recognizing the significance of this wedge in the heart of their Arab enclave, they concentrated all their forces in those fifteen square kilometers stretching between Nahariya, the farthest edge of the partially populated Jewish region, and Hanita.

The jarring reports from Europe worsened. By now Jews were social pariahs. Newspapers were full of alarming stories about Europe, and a considerable segment of the population in Palestine had relatives there. Hence the settlement of Hanita also served to boost morale. They prepared maps and arms, generators and building material. The stockade was built, then taken apart and crated so it could be reassembled quickly. On the night of the actual settlement in the area, a caravan of some seventy trucks crawled along the road up the rocky mountain. Hundreds of other people infiltrated across the wadis and hastily set up tower and stockade.

On that same night, the first night in Hanita, all of a sudden at midnight hundreds of weapons fired simultaneously in a synchronized blast. The well-armed attackers stormed. On that first night Hanita was almost wiped out. Yossi took a stand and fired accurately in different directions to give the impression there were many posts. Jacob Berger, Yossi's boyhood friend who stood alongside him, was hit in the foot and became the first fatality of Hanita. Today it is difficult to grasp how death could have followed such an injury; after all, Haifa was not far away and had a hospital with good doctors. People risked their lives transporting the wounded from the area to the temporary hospital in Nahariya—some of them got wounded during the transport—and then to Haifa. Despite all this, Berger and ten other men died from blood poisoning due to wounds that had become infected.

During the months that Yossi remained in Hanita, the Arabs continued their attacks within the framework of what they considered the key to their struggle against Jewish settlement, given the increased Jewish readiness to fight. The spot became more and more isolated on account of the tightening siege. There was nobody to come and rescue them in an emergency. It was hard to deliver food there, and the British were trying to prevent the delivery of arms. Whatever did get through had to be concealed.

One day a car with three young men set out from Hanita, bound for Nahariya. When shots rang out, Yossi jumped onto a pickup truck and zoomed along an improvised road. He spotted the overturned car, approached, and came under fire. Together with his command, he leaped into a ditch on his right, crawled forward, and found the three murdered boys. A battle began. While still shooting, he heard a cry: "Help! Help!" A boy, just a moment ago sitting beside him as they sped in the truck, was hit. Yossi crawled to him under an inferno of whistling bullets, found him bleeding profusely, and pulled him to the protected side of the road.

It was Passover 1938. The fields were enormous embroidered carpets of anemones. To this day, more than sixty years afterward, when spring arrives and, along with it, anemones bloom, the smell of blood fills his nostrils.

Chapter Three

One Friday night a car arrived in Hanita unescorted. Inside sat an older man wearing a British military cap and a rumpled civilian suit. He was armed with a rifle and had a pistol under his belt. He slumped a bit, and his appearance evoked the image of an ascetic priest. His blue eyes, thinness, and gait accorded him an aura of mystery. The man held a Bible in his hand, with an attached note from Chaim Weizmann and a letter from Ben-Gurion that introduced him as "Captain Orde Charles Wingate, a great friend" and requested that they take good care of him and cooperate with him.

When he was invited into the dining hall, he refused to eat what he was served and asked for a raw onion. Until then the Haganah was used to tidy, spick-and-span British officers who generally treated them with boastful arrogance. And here was a slovenly dressed British officer chewing a raw onion and displaying bad manners. His face was gaunt and pale, his expression piercing. His eyes were sunk in their sockets and glistened like polished steel. He ate the onion slowly. Yossi thought that after such an arduous trip he would request to recuperate. But he did not do so. Instead he simply took charge and instructed, rather than asked, that he be given a tour. They spent several hours on an exhausting tour, and upon their return he ushered them into one of the rooms. There were no chairs, so they sat on the floor. He opened with a lecture about his plans and, for demonstration purposes, inserted matchsticks in the cracks between the tiles.

The next morning they went out with him on a tour of another area. They were surprised by the way he read maps, which was, in Yossi's words, the way a gifted musician read the score of a symphony. They were unaccustomed to intensity like his and did not ask any questions. Yossi, the child of a small Jerusalem neighborhood, felt that this man, with his international aura and rich adventures, possessed magnetic power; pure, aristocratic, restrained force; a callous, charismatic innocence. After a short while they were already performing with feverish excitement under his command night after night. They'd go up to the border, steal deep into Lebanese territory for the first time in the chronicles of the Arab-Jewish conflict, and reach the villages from where shots were fired at night, and Wingate would peer through his binoculars and nod his head. Yossi studied and learned from this wild, primitive leopard how to approach a village against the wind so the dogs would not pick up the scent and start to bark, and how to compete in an area he had never been before. When they asked Wingate how he recognized which way to go and what tactics to use, he answered quite simply, "It's all written in the Bible. The places, the tactics—they're all in the Bible. In *Proverbs* it is written, 'With cunning you shall wage war.'"

Wingate, the son of a distinguished Scottish family, was the one who conceived and initiated the British army's commando practices involving quick night raids to exploit the element of surprise, and the use of small units, swift and well drilled. As a boy he had ridden a bike in the Alps in order to retrace the route taken by Hannibal, whom he worshiped. He relied upon the military judgment of the heroes in the Bible. He linked them to the landscape he knew from Scripture and considered them his teachers. He turned to Weizmann and recommended himself as general of the Jewish army, because he believed in the return of the Jewish people to their historical homeland, and that was how he came to Hanita.

The key to Wingate's warm and unique relationship with Yossi, and the profound bond that developed between them, lay in Yossi's courage. In one of the raids with Wingate, Yossi entered a village inside Lebanon. Their forces were assaulted, and Yossi wiped out a complete unit with hand grenades. From then on Wingate called him "the Bomber" and recommended him for a medal. The Englishman loved reticent heroes, and he admired Yossi's version of bravery—his grasp of the secret of restraint, his instinct for knowing just when to express feelings—as well as Yossi's gutsy adventurousness, his unflagging sense of responsibility, his integrity. When they learned that Haim Shturman, the fearless fighter whom Wingate loved and revered, had been killed at the Jordan River, Wingate called upon Yossi to accompany him to Kibbutz Ain-Harod.

Shturman had been part of the first group of revolutionaries to arrive at the beginning of the century and defend themselves rather than hire out unreliable Arab or Druze militiamen to do it for them. He was a legendary fighter known for his belief in finding a way to live in peace with the Arabs he fought against.

At the cemetery, facing the mountains of Gilboa, one of the most exquisite sites in the land of Israel, during the quiet, restrained funeral, Yossi watched Wingate salute Shturman as they placed the gray basalt stone on his grave. In time, many such stones would cover members of Shturman's family.

From the valley rose the sweet aroma of blossoms, and the chirping of birds floated in the air. At night they all entered the home of Haim's wife, Atara, a calm and reserved woman, one of the founders of Hashomer, the Jewish Watchman Organization of Yossi's boyhood. She was there with her son Moshe, Yossi's beloved pupil in Hanita, who would get killed in the War of Independence. After losing her husband and her son, she would also lose two grandsons, one in the war for the Sinai desert and another during the Yom Kippur War, on Green Island near the Suez Canal.

Atara would spend her whole life on her kibbutz, surrounded by the wives of her sons and their children and busying herself among them. In that house Yossi felt as if he were adopted, as if he finally belonged. Among these people who stubbornly clung to the hard mud of the valley, he was part of the family, in a home he never really had. Standing opposite her, Yossi felt how the Nomads, Yitzhak Sadeh, Hanita—all of it was somehow planted in this landscape, in this modest house, in this woman. A destitute but noble queen of the tribe of proud wretches, bereft of four of her men from various battles of one very long war. Atara's legacy was the nostalgic poem "To My Country" by Rachel:

> *I have not sung you, my country,*
> *Not brought glory to your name,*
> *With the great deeds of a hero*
> *Or the spoils a battle yields.*
>
> *Modest are the gifts I bring you,*
> *I know this, mother.*
> *Modest, I know, the offerings*
> *Of your daughter:*
> *Only an outburst of song*
> *On a day when the light flares up,*
> *Only a silent tear for your poverty.*

These were the very words that would be sung a few years later on the deck of the *Knesset Israel* by a concentration-camp whore of the SS, though this melancholy pastoral poem never had her in mind.

Yossi sat in Atara's home with Wingate, the unruly, mystical genius, who also gazed at the brave woman with affection. Wingate the Englishman felt the way Yossi did, as if he had been born there. Atara laughed. And Yossi thought: Atara, the Hebrew word for crown—a queen's crown of thorns and gold. The tribal queen of the desperate who believed everything was all right, everything had to happen as it did, everything was worth the price of pain, and a semi-Hasidic devotion could grace a situation that was savage and practically stripped of hope.

Wingate, a Puritan by education and ascetic in conduct, would often quote Disraeli; though he had left the Jewish faith and his books only cagily touched upon his origins, Disraeli wrote in a book called *Tancred*, "The vineyards of Israel have ceased to exist. But the eternal law enjoins the children of Israel still to celebrate the vintage. A race that persists in celebrating their vintage that have no fruits to gather, will regain their vineyards."

Subsequently Wingate proposed to General Montgomery, then the British commander of northern Palestine, that he establish what became known as the Special Night Squads (SNS), using fighters from Sadeh's field companies (FOSH). These units would patrol the border in an effort to block arms smuggling and protect the vital Iraq–Haifa oil line, which the Arabs had started to sabotage on a regular basis, causing great damage to the British war effort. Montgomery needed the Jewish fighters of Palestine and accepted his proposal.

According to an intelligence report, an Arab gang had organized at a distance of about seven kilometers from the border and was ready to attack the pipeline. Wingate notified Yossi: "We're heading to meet them halfway." It was night. They went single file, Wingate first, half-blind and relying on other senses. The plan was this: When they encountered the approaching gang, Wingate would raise a stick, from which hung a small lantern with a red light inside. At once the two sections behind him would leap to either side of the path, he himself would clear the way, and the gang would fall into the trap. The operation succeeded, and immediately afterward the British authorized the establishment of the night squads.

In another operation they stormed a village and conducted a search. Fire rained down on them from the infiltrators, who fled and stationed themselves on the hilltops. They returned fire. The gang was surprised by the intensity of fire and began to retreat toward the Kishon River, but as they neared the Kishon they were pinned down by fire from the second squad sent out earlier to block their escape. Despite the blow, the Arabs managed to break through to the west, where they met the third squad, set up by Wingate, and were badly hurt in the crossfire. Arms were captured, as well as valuable documents proving the involvement of several Arab countries in supplying the gangs with equipment and commanders.

The operations came more frequently and became more ruthless. The Arabs complained to the British about Wingate's brutality and harsh punitive measures. Even members of the field squads whose organization was based on the Nomads, and within whose framework Yossi was now active, complained that during the raids on Bedouin encampments Wingate would behave with extreme viciousness and fire mercilessly. Wingate believed in the principle of surprise in punishment, which was designed to confine the gangs to their villages. More than once he had lined up rioters in a row and shot them in cold blood. Wingate did not try to justify himself; weapons and war never can be pure. In one of the battles against rioters who had set fire to the pipeline, a gang was captured. The oil spurted in a gigantic fiery stream, and Wingate grabbed one of them and shoved his head in the oil. As Yossi was about to do likewise, Wingate restrained him with a half smile: "It's not worth your doing it. In the end we'll leave, and you'll remain here with them."

On the heels of the Arab complaints and the political shift of the British, who were fearful of the increased Jewish immigration, the British General Staff began to plague Wingate. His excessively warm relationship with the Jews and his treatment of the Bible as Jewish property was out of step with the political position adopted at that time. It was decided to reassign him to Egypt. On the eve of his departure he drove to Haifa with two bottles of whiskey. He met the commander of Haganah intelligence and informed him of the contents of the "White Paper" that was to be published that year. Wingate delivered his parting speech to the Haganah commanders in Hebrew. His placement in Egypt caused him great pain. He was a gifted commander, devout in his faith and farsighted. Wingate expected to stand at the head of the Jewish army. Out of despair, he cut his throat with a razor after he arrived in Egypt and only by chance was saved. He was flown to England, recovered, was assigned to Ethiopia, and fought on the side of Emperor Haile Selassie with units modeled on those he had set up in Hanita. He reenacted the raids he had led in Galilee and Lebanon, this time against the Italian army, penetrating deep inside enemy lines. On the wake of his successes, he was transferred to Burma. When Churchill recognized his exceptional ability to conceive, train, and build a model small army, mobile and bold, Wingate was promoted to the rank of general, but he perished in a plane accident during a storm at night. When Yossi heard of this, as he listened to a BBC news broadcast, he sat alone and mourned not only the outstanding commander, but also the man he loved.

After Hanita, Yossi was appointed commander of the FOSH unit in the Tel Mond bloc. There he learned to sharpen his eyes in anticipation of the greatest and roughest night of his life, which would occur eight years later, on two of the largest blockade-running ships in the history of Aliyah Beth, or, as he put it, the greatest Jewish exodus since the Exodus from Egypt. He learned how to protect thousands of people by means of loyalty, integrity, agility, and vigilance.

It was winter then. Arabs had laid mines in the unpaved dirt roads. Settlements in the area lived in constant dread. People were killed and maimed. It was Yossi's responsibility to comb the roads before any buses or trucks went out. The living quarters of the unit he commanded were exposed to the elements. Warm clothes and blankets were unavailable. A unit of forty men shared ten overcoats and went out early each morning before the buses and trucks left for Tel Aviv. He and his men lay with their heads dangling over the hood of the truck. They looked like a cluster of grapes. And with eyes glued to the loose soil, they tried to discover land mines hidden in the muddy deceptive sand and search for footprints in the path.

This was an impromptu operation calling for intuition and boldness, and it succeeded only thanks to sharp eyes, eyes that memorized every bump in the road and could immediately detect any lurking danger.

Chapter Four

Wingate had been correct. In 1939 the White Paper was indeed issued—on the anniversary of Kristallnacht and four years after the promulgation of the Nuremberg Laws. The earth burned under the feet of the Jews. The United States piled up more and more obstacles for Jewish refugees streaming to its shores and, like other countries, gave asylum almost exclusively to Jewish scientists. The British insisted on locking the gates of Palestine, so the Arabs got what they wanted and ceased their revolt. A nearly total ban on immigration of Jews to Palestine prevailed, despite their increasing numbers, and likewise strict limitations were imposed on the purchase of land. Nazi parades were held on the streets of German Templar colonies all across Palestine, and Arabs applauded. At that time, under the command of Shaul Avigur, the chief of Haganah intelligence, Yossi headed a department in Jerusalem that prepared files on intelligence officers of the British CID and on Jewish collaborators in their service. Some were executed. The atmosphere was tense. Yossi went without sleep; rather than punish Jewish traitors, what he really wanted to do at that historical moment was save Jews. He asked to be transferred for sea training.

There was a bad feeling in Palestine. The Arabs didn't fight anymore. Britain's fortified wall against Jewish immigration was sufficiently massive and delivered impressive results. Yossi wanted to save Jews—something barely attempted—but he wanted as well to take part in the world war. He was torn. By

fighting in the war to save Jews, was he also in some sense coop-
erating with the British in a joint enterprise? He became restless.
Jewish organizations in Palestine collaborated with the British in
their fight against the Germans; even the undergound groups
participated and declared a cease-fire in their efforts to sabotage
the British presence in Palestine.

Thus, contrary to the unyielding position of his commanders that it was necessary to establish and maintain a Jewish force
in Palestine in the face of what could be expected in future,
Yossi—no longer the reliable and obedient young man he had
been until now—decided to join the thousands of other Jews of
Palestine in enlisting in the British army. At a staff meeting of the
Haganah in Jerusalem, Yossi was declared a deserter and tried
in absentia for dereliction of duty.

An expert marksman, Yossi hoped to serve in the Royal Air
Force on bombing missions. The Palestinian passport in his possession, however, did not persuade the recruiters. When he was
asked if he knew how to drive a car, he answered in the positive
and was stationed in Egypt, in a supplies unit of the 32nd Air-
borne Division that included three squadrons of sixty planes, all
based in Abukir, near Alexandria. In mid-1940 he set out, along
with an endless caravan, across the western desert to the area of
combat in the Libyan sands. The journey took three months. En
route they were attacked without pause. After he returned to
Egypt he was transferred with his squadron to Greece, in a convoy of ships that was bombed by German Stuka planes. A British soldier was killed right next to Yossi and was buried at sea.
The burial ceremony made a deep impression on Yossi, and from
then on he was of the mind that a man ought to be buried in the
spot where he died. All those aboard came to the deck and stood
at attention. The commanders wrapped the body in white linen
and draped the British flag over it. The priest and the captain
eulogized the deceased. And at the sound of the words "We commit thy body to the deep," the body slipped into the high seas.
The ship didn't stop for even a moment.

In Greece, the squadron was concentrated in a base not far from the capital. Evenings, Yossi went to Athens. With a friend from Jerusalem he visited the amphitheater on the mountain and saw a production of *Antigone,* which proved to be an awesome experience. He felt a kinship with Greek tragedy, in which all is predetermined and there is no happy ending. The saving grace is the act itself, which in any case remains pointless. Whatever happens *must* happen. At the end of the play he was unable to stand up. He felt like a stone from Jerusalem in an alien land. The Greeks maintained that in a godless world, paltry man is the arbiter, even in defeat, and Yossi would come to embody that. He identified with the glorious battle in which three hundred Greeks died fighting against tens of thousands of Persian soldiers. He felt a kinship with the Greek soldier who ran to Athens after the battle of Marathon, to report the victory over Darius, but died from exhaustion as he reached the gates of the city, having run thirty-five kilometers nonstop.

When the squadron got transferred to northern Greece on the Yugoslavian border, the Germans responded with ferocity. Forty German planes attacked the ships, and all those aboard were forced to jump overboard and swim ashore, with no weapons, food, or extra clothes. They waited until a pair of destroyers picked them up and took them to Crete. Two days after they departed from Crete, the island was overrun by a force of German paratroopers. Whoever had not been evacuated in time got captured.

As a result of the intense bombardment at sea, Yossi's right eardrum ruptured and he permanently lost his hearing on that side. The injury caused a serious ear infection and fever. When his pain worsened he was given a week's furlough. Instead of entering the infirmary, he traveled from Corfu to Tel Aviv. Upon arrival, he headed at once for Cafe Atara, Yitzhak Sadeh's headquarters. Sadeh looked at him as if they had parted just a moment ago and said: "It's a good thing you're here. You're coming with me to Haifa. Too bad you didn't arrive two days earlier.

Cooperation with the British has resumed, and we are supposed to sabotage the oil refineries in Tripoli. We've sent a ship with twenty-three commandos. I wanted to appoint you commander because Spector was wounded, but I had no choice, you weren't around. Tsvi Spector got the command anyway."

Sadeh and Yossi left Tel Aviv and stayed at one of the hotels on the Carmel. From there, all night, they peered through binoculars across the bay and waited. There was no sign of a ship, and to this day its fate remains unknown.

A week later Yossi was sent out to transport a truck. For four days he drove at the head of a pioneer unit through the desert until he reached Baghdad, en route to the Caucasian front to aid the Red Army. But when the appointed time arrived for him to depart, the operation was canceled and he was ordered to proceed to Singapore in the war against Japan. This operation was also canceled at the last moment, when it was decided to redirect his unit to the western desert, to the war against the German army, which had advanced under the command of Field Marshal Erwin Rommel.

Yossi again submitted a request for active duty as a bomber pilot and was again rejected owing to the injury to his ear. The doctors wanted to operate on him in a hospital in Gaza, but he refused. The disappearance of his friend Spector made him want to return home, so he requested and received an honorable discharge from the British army and was decorated with the medal awarded servicemen wounded in action. At the end of 1941 he returned to Haganah headquarters in Tel Aviv, and the issue of his desertion was forgotten.

In Palestine, anxiety bordering on panic prevailed. More than a third of the Jewish community were refugees from the Nazis. On the radio they heard the joyous outbursts and boasts of the commanders of the German army, which was advancing rapidly across the western desert. Rommel had conquered North Africa by storm, and the English were in retreat.

Except for the British army in Egypt, nothing separated the Germans from Palestine. Like the majority of Arabs, the Egyptians were pro-German and hoped for victory over Britain. It was well understood in Palestine what it meant for a small Jewish community surrounded by Arabs, most of them pro-Nazi, to fall into German hands. In such a case there was no real chance for escape, and people saw with sorrowful eyes the terrible slaughter awaiting them and tried to do something about it. They began to conceive of another Masada, this time on Mt. Carmel.

Immediately upon his return, Yossi fit into the framework of the action called "Musa Dagh in Palestine." He trained forces of the Haganah for this impossible war. He implemented Sadeh's principle, which would subsequently guide the future Israel Defense Force: "We have no Maginot Line, we cannot allow ourselves any tranquillity or glitch even in time of peace." Thus Sadeh was the first to formulate the axiom that Israelis had no place to retreat to, not even for tactical reasons, and their only defense was offense.

Meanwhile plans were drawn up for the evacuation of the centers of population. A general Arab uprising was taken into consideration, and the high commissioner of Palestine notified Shaul Avigur, the head of the Haganah, in no uncertain terms that if the English were forced to retreat—and that seemed likely—they wouldn't lift a finger to protect the Jewish community of Palestine. Yossi helped to map the route of tactical retreat across Mt. Gilboa and, farther, across Beit Shaan. They trained small guerrilla units that would remain behind enemy lines. There was a general consensus that it was necessary to fight even if it was hopeless. They clearly knew that the prospects of withstanding Rommel's well-equipped, massive army were next to zero, but the mere act of preparation contributed a certain confidence.

After Rommel was famously crushed by General Montgomery at El Alamein and the theater of war switched to Europe, the British decided to enlist Palestine Jews to take part in the sabotage units that would work in cooperation with British intelligence. According to the plan, a number of commandos who, along with Yossi, had taken various courses taught by the British would head for Yugoslavia, and from there to the countries of Eastern Europe, on a mission of sabotage and information gathering.

Now twenty-four years old, Yossi stood at the threshold of a mission from which he had little chance of returning alive. He was meant to sink a German ship on the Danube behind the Iron Curtain, between Yugoslavia and Romania, paralyzing movement along the river and making it harder for the Germans to navigate to the Straits. Yet, tranquillity and serenity engulfed him on the eve of his departure for the mission, which, from any angle, was an act of suicide.

In the end, the operation was never carried out. The British became suspicious and canceled it at the last minute—without warning the Palestine Jews or coordinating with them. Apparently they didn't want to place the requisite means of transport into the hands of the Jewish community, fearing that the Jews would trick them and smuggle in refugees who were still trying, again and again, to reach Palestine on rickety ships, most of which sank. For the Jews, this act of British contempt amounted to a terrible betrayal.

Chapter Five

As the Second World War was winding down, pressure from Jews wanting to immigrate to Palestine mounted. The British stubbornly refused to open the gates. Although the rage in the Jewish community of Palestine soared, for the most part it amounted to apathy and tight-lipped guardedness: the British were indeed choking off immigration to Palestine, but at the same time they were waging a war to the death against the Germans.

This was after everyone had already heard what "happened" but before the horror sank in. Similarly, they did not hearken to the cries of Shmuel Siegelbaum, the Bund representative in the government of Free Poland stationed in London, who incessantly broadcast his reports about the slaughter of hundreds of thousands. Despite his precise information, nobody paid attention to the warnings he issued with ever greater frequency, ever greater fury, ever greater pain. Given the impermeability of his listeners along with the burden of the horrifying facts he endured hour by hour, Siegelbaum, heartbroken, committed suicide.

In 1942, when the U.S. State Department finally publicized the meaning of "the final solution," the *New York Times* published—on page ten—that two and a half million Jews had already been exterminated. *Time, Life,* and most of the newspapers except for the Yiddish press, kept their mouths shut till the very end of the war. The church remained silent. Mute.

At American consulates, tens of thousands of Jews registered for asylum. The number of requests was so high at times that it would probably have taken more than fifty years for any petitioner's turn to come up. In New York, noisy Nazi parades were held. The anti-Semitic priest Charles Coughlin, who transmitted his doctrines over the airwaves, had nearly three million loyal listeners to heed his weekly slanders against American Jews, whose situation was shaky anyway; the majority of big employers, from the telephone company to the automobile industry, refused to hire them. Many establishments hung signs: "Jews and dogs not admitted."

For America, Middle East interests took precedence over the plight of the perishing Jews of Europe. This was before the bitter truth had penetrated the national Jewish consciousness that saving the world from Hitler did not include saving the Jews. As Ze'ev Jabotinsky put it, "Jews were not on the world's daily agenda."

In October of 1945 Ben-Gurion returned from a tour of the transit camps in Europe, one of the worst experiences of his life. With a touch of regret he repeated—this time with intensified anger and helplessness—what he had proclaimed in 1942 during an emergency session of Zionists at the Biltmore Hotel in New York: "Without a state, there can be no revival for the remnant of the Jewish people." In November 1945 this terrible iniquity of the absence of the Jews on the world's agenda transformed into a powerful catalyst that altered Jewish history and reality once and for all. Dreams of a Jewish state, in the past always an impotent quasi mantra, now became a strategic imperative.

The struggle against the British was renewed at the end of the war once the gates of Palestine were almost totally shut. Many Jews in Palestine had family members "over there" who perished or disappeared or were now waiting in transit camps in Europe for permission to immigrate. A feeling of guilt was rife in Palestine. They beat their breasts, for they'd actually had it good when they'd worked for the British, building their military camps and airfields, and had not protested when 150,000 Polish and Yugoslavian refugees, all non-Jews, were brought to live in the Middle East and Palestine until the end of the war, while Jews were forbidden to come. In the United States Jews began to regret having done so little for their brethren out of fear of anti-Semitism in America. Such anti-Semitism was evident in many ways, including a survey conducted in 1942 after the destruction of the Jews became known, in which Jews were shown to be considered the third greatest threat to America after Germany and Japan. The only active group in the United States was that of Hillel Kook (then Peter Bergson). It encountered opposition but responded forcefully. Kook did not hold back any effort on behalf of Jews all over the world. For his work, the playwright Ben Hecht called him a "Man of History." But Kook and his associates could accomplish very little. From the balconies of Tel Aviv the sea appeared full of shadows and suspicions, yet empty of ships.

To protest the eviction of a small ship filled with illegal immigrants from the shores of Palestine, an extensive operation was launched involving the entire community. The Haganah and the Palmach attacked nearly two hundred road junctions, railway tracks, and buildings connected with coastal defense, temporarily paralyzing the British in one concentrated effort.

In 1945 the land was rife with competing factions. Haganah headquarters learned that the Freedom Fighters for Israel, also known as the Stern Gang, was out to kill Weizmann because of his politics of compromise. Yossi was asked to accompany Weizmann as his bodyguard and as the Haganah contact. Weizmann still believed in persuasion and the existence of common Anglo-Jewish interests, relying on the Balfour Declaration, which apparently only the Jews took seriously. But at the same time, other winds blew among the Jews—actively anti-British ones. Weizmann was defeated by Ben-Gurion, who finally placed him in a golden cage by appointing him president. Of the Jewish mediators of this era, Weizmann was the last Titan.

Yossi Harel was at Weizmann's side all the time. Although he was a Ben-Gurion devotee and in touch with Weizmann's ideological foes, Yossi became his confidant. The obvious question was how could Yossi, a disciple of Yitzhak Sadeh and a fighter without illusions, befriend Weizmann, the aristocratic compromiser who believed in negotiation? How could a young man who headed for the desert with his friends in the youth movement in order to experience the scorched earth and observe birds of prey, who wanted to become a part of the shards and the rocks and felt they were the descendants of kings of yore, not of Jews from the ghetto, a young man who loved to sit among monks in picturesque monasteries high up on cliffs in the desert, to look straight into the eyes of eagles, meet Bedouins, and speak their language, a man active in the Haganah, young and vigorous—how could he love Weizmann, the sober, restrained rationalist who knew the landscapes of Palestine and its byways only from reading books, a man who flustered at the sight of the Jews of Peki'in who never left the land, Jews who prepared a festive meal for him, shouted, kneaded dough, and sang?! And he was the man who said in Yiddish, on his way back to Rehovot: "Oi, how lucky we were to be exiled from here!" How could Yossi be loyal to such a cautious, elegiac, occasionally obsequious old man? How did the two of them develop such a strong bond of affection?

That was Yossi's gift. He was not only able to internalize two opposing sides; in him they complemented one another. This quality was very much born of his Jerusalem childhood, which taught him to bridge contradictions.

But Weizmann saw Yossi's activism as an imprudent and ill-considered step toward transforming Zionism into something brutal. Why, then, did Weizmann rely so much on the young man known for adventurism? What developed between the two resembled an unspoken father-son relationship, in the wake of the death of Weizmann's son while serving as a pilot in the Royal Air Force. Perhaps, too, the relationship was in part a consequence of Yossi's capacity to gaze directly into the eyes of a mature man and comprehend the distress of someone who was every inch a leader, from head to toe, maybe the greatest Zionist leader, who had already begun to fade as in some Greek tragedy and turn into the victim of betrayal, though he couldn't even fathom the concept of betrayal.

After the Jews began streaming by the thousands to the shores of the Mediterranean Sea in hopes of reaching Palestine, Weizmann remained even more isolated in his inability to comprehend illegal immigration. He wrapped himself in a radiant sheath of loneliness.

In 1946, a short while before Yossi was about to leave him, the two of them went to Haifa to visit Weizmann's brother, Yehiel, the father of Ezer (who would go on to become the president of Israel in 1993). Yossi had maintained continuous contact with Shaul Avigur, whom Weizmann disparagingly called "your people" to include all his more military-oriented friends. Avigur had been present a few weeks earlier at the capture of the *Henrietta Szold* in Haifa Bay. The commander of the ship was Samek, Yossi's friend. When the ship was taken, blood was spilled. The English had fought with red-hot fury. After the British destroyer *Ajax* rammed the boat, the soldiers roughed up the refugees. The *Ajax* had become a symbol for Samek and his friends during the world war, when it trounced the enormous German battleship *Graf Spee* in a famous sea battle, a defeat that caused the commander to commit suicide. Now its sailors were fighting against Jewish refugees. Yossi was instrumental in bringing Samek to Yehiel's house; Samek was flustered at first, then began to speak up. Weizmann sat and listened as if hypnotized, and Yossi felt as if every word were a dagger in Weizmann's heart.

On their way back to Rehovot, Weizmann still would not speak. They passed by Givat Olga, where the British had installed the largest radar station in Palestine to detect illegal ships. As the stiff, restrained Weizmann peered outside the window for a moment, he was finally able to bring himself to speak. In a tone Yossi had never heard before, he said: "Why don't you tell your people to blow up that station?!" He blushed and said no more. A short while later, after they blew up the station, Weizmann rushed to condemn the action for causing shock and a flood of threats from the British side.

At first glance, the combination Sadeh-Weizmann seemed an impossibility, but in Yossi they complemented one another. For Sadeh, war was the romantic coup of the unknown, powerlessness become power. He was a split revolutionary, a Jewish scholar turned secular who painfully deciphered the meaning of Weizmann's monitored manners. Both were fastidious about their external appearance, and both suffered on that account. Sadeh looked like an old man while he was still young. Weizmann looked like a delicate suit of clothes compared with the rough sabra pioneers who came in contact with him.

Both of them became outdated before they accomplished their goals. In a way, that was why Yossi linked both of them with the essence of his Jerusalem boyhood, when he had seen Hasidim dancing opposite dervishes who flogged themselves with iron chains and heard Arab muezzins calling for prayer opposite women who wept on the Mount of Olives. Yossi had, therefore, quite a few fathers: Sadeh, Wingate, Avigur, and Weizmann, in addition to his biological father, whom he loved very much but rarely got to see.

Yossi conducted a stubborn romance with illegal immigration. He wanted to play a role in it, knowing that he was suitable for the task. But he also knew that Shaul Avigur, the commander in chief of this great enterprise, wanted to send him to bring large ships, having come to the conclusion that indeed Yossi was the man for an undertaking of such magnitude as illegal immigration. Avigur knew Yossi from the Nomads and Hanita. He had taken note of him during the unloading of immigrants from the *Dora* on the coast of Shfaim in 1939, when Tsvi Spector, his boyhood friend, brought the ship and Yossi had come to help out. These two idealistic Zionist cowboys—who at the time did not know this would be their last meeting—worked together with skillful teamwork and executed the disembarkment with exemplary discipline.

Avigur saw and was impressed. Here was a man who understood restraint and economy, but at the same time had been dubbed "the Bomber" by Wingate for his courage and fearlessness in performing solo military missions. He wanted this youth from Jerusalem who was not so quick to become one of the crowd. He wanted him in order to forestall any tragedies between the "fast draws" and the "responsible quietists." Whatever Yossi gained from the impossible blend of his mother, father, Sadeh, Wingate, and Weizmann, this entire package Shaul Avigur wished to acquire for the refugee rescue operation.

Shaul Avigur came to Yossi in the wake of the event that left him with a broken heart for the rest of his life. In 1940 two ships—the *Pacific* and the *Milos*—arrived in Haifa from the shores of Europe filled with Jewish refugees. The ships, purchased by private individuals, held 2,500 illegal immigrants altogether, and both were captured. A third, the *Atlantic,* was still on its way to Haifa. The British lost their temper and raged against the Jews for coming to Palestine, which was closed to them, and brought another ship, the *Patria,* planning to load it with the detained illegal immigrants and transport them to the island of Mauritius.

When the *Patria* was ready to pull up anchor with hundreds of refugees on its decks, Shaul Avigur and the staff of Aliyah Beth decided to sabotage the ship so it would not be able to sail. The explosion was scheduled to go off when all the refugees would be on deck for review. According to the plan, at that very moment a demonstration would take place, and while the police emerged from their daily inspection of the cabins below, the refugees would exploit the confusion and leap into the water. The detonated mine would bore a small hole into the side of the ship, damaging it and preventing the deportation. But as it turned out, the mine exploded before people reached the deck, and the ship was damaged much more severely than planned. It capsized and then suddenly split in two. The refugees were caught in the middle.

Nobody had considered the possibility that the ship's side was rusty and rotten, or that a tiny explosion could cause such extensive damage. And, of course, no one imagined the British would lock the ship's doors. Hundreds of Jews drowned in front of Haifa. They could not be rescued from the holding pens that sealed them. The British jumped from the sinking ship without releasing those still imprisoned. Crushed against the locked doors as they tried in vain to open the gates, 267 refugees died from asphyxiation. Just one Britisher, Henas Wendell, tried to unlock the gates and save them, but the waters washed over him, too.

The deportation itself demonstrated British cunning and determination to block Jewish immigration. At the Atlit detention camp, where refugees who survived the sinking of the ship were taken, 1,645 adults and children waited. Refugees on the *Atlantic* got transported on a different ship to the torrid island of Mauritius, whose climate was terribly harsh. The British stormed the small camp near the Haifa–Tel Aviv highway and forcibly dragged women who tried to resist, tearing out hair and earrings along with earlobes. Among the British, some felt ashamed at the sight of the fierce reaction against the displaced refugees who had just escaped from drowning. But most of the police and soldiers acted like brutes, because of "the problems the Jews made for them." The clash with the refugees lasted eight consecutive hours, until they were all assembled half-naked, bruised, and bloody. In a fury that included beatings and lashings with whips, the survivors were loaded onto a ship and deported to the island of Mauritius. The journey was draining. Upon their arrival, they found a remote camp in the middle of a desert. In this tropical island camp they were housed in huts made of wobbly tin that blazed in the strong sun. Men and women were separated for more than a year and a half. Typhus and other diseases spread among them. On August 11, 1945, when they were released from Mauritius, they left behind 128 graves for those who could not withstand the diseases, filth, and abuse of the British. On the journey back, two others died from severe injuries they had sustained earlier.

From the point of view of rough and reserved Shaul Avigur, the torment he endured in the aftermath of the *Patria* affair was the greatest tragedy of his life, though it also became the yardstick by which he would conduct himself in future. Never again would he permit improvisations. Never again would he allow his commandos to engage in a mission without thoroughly checking every single detail beforehand. The ascetic man of secrecy and alienation, who could not disclose his feelings, trembled like a driven leaf from then on, fearful that something might happen to the Jewish children waiting for the ships. After the *Patria* affair, an endless stream of pleas to relieve the suffering of the refugees reached the shores of Palestine. The British refused to listen. They claimed it was forbidden to show the Arabs they submitted to the Jews. In the eyes of Avigur, the wonder worker, every ship holding illegal immigrants, even if captured, was a battering ram smashing the wall of Jerusalem or, more correctly, the wall of the White Paper.

Like Ben-Gurion, Avigur was a man without illusions. Already in 1934, in cooperation with the revisionist immigration operation that managed to dispatch several ships, he tried to help Jews escape from Europe, but again and again he found himself up against the obstinate British, the indifference of America as well as the rest of the free world, and even the lack of enthusiasm of some Jewish agencies in Palestine. Intuitively, before anybody else, he knew from reading maps without bias or illusion that, during the war, America really didn't see the Jews as its partner and practically shut its gates in their faces. Saving Jews was not one of the manifest goals of the Allies. At war's end, when Jewish refugees began pouring from that hell, whether to the land of Israel or to the shores of America, the gates everywhere shut even tighter. Ernest Bevin, the British foreign minister, urged the Americans to accept into their borders four hundred thousand Jewish refugees so Britain could remain in Palestine and contain

communism, which was spreading rapidly in the Middle East—
that was his way of solving the problem of Palestine. But the
Americans refused.

In the course of the war, any evidence of the extermination
campaign was destroyed by the censors and redefined as aiding
the enemy. Hollywood was asked not to make war films that
mentioned the Jew. The churches remained silent. The American
papers hid the news of the slaughter. The Voice of America, like
the BBC, was prevented from reporting what was happening in
the camps and ghettos, so a Jew residing in a small town awaiting his fate would not know for sure what was occurring in some
other town. America was swept up in a wave of unprecedented
anti-Semitism. Through worldwide diplomatic representatives,
the American Foreign Office toyed with tens of thousands of
Jews holding green cards obtained with difficulty. In a national
questionnaire conducted at that time, more than 50 percent of
Americans said that Jews were "different from us," should be
"restricted," and were a fifth column. If the United States had
merely warned Hitler that the extermination of Jews was against
American policy and denounced it as a war crime, the Nazis
would have been more cautious. After all, they took Western
protests on other, much simpler issues quite seriously.

In 1944, Horthy, the leader of Hungary, who despite his pact
with Nazi Germany did not lend a hand to the extermination of
Jews, was removed from power. Spring that year was especially
lovely. Intoxicating aromas hung in the air. The Germans invaded
Hungary and began a massive extermination. Daily, twelve
thousand people were transported by trains to Auschwitz. The
extermination was performed with astonishing enthusiasm, in
consideration of the fact that Hungary was a loyal ally of Germany and the Red Army was already banging on the doors of a
German empire starting to shrink.

Even then, Roosevelt, Churchill, and Stalin refused to ad-
monish the Germans to halt the killing. It looked as if the Nazis
thought they were working on behalf of the West as well. In 1944,

when the extermination of the Jews of Hungary commenced, a strong ultimatum was issued by the Allied foreign ministers: Molotov, Eden, and Hale. It included an explicit warning to the Germans that if gas was used against citizens in the occupied areas, the Allies would respond proportionately and with equal firepower against German cities. Jewish organizations tried to influence the Americans and the British to incorporate the Jews in the ultimatum, but the Jews as always were considered enemy subjects. Thus, even when President Roosevelt warned the Germans that any use of gas against the armed forces of the Allies would lead to a comparable counterattack, he rejected out of hand the advice to include the Jews in the warning.

On his visit to America that very year, the British foreign minister, Anthony Eden, told Jewish representatives when they asked for his help in transporting several thousand Jews from Bulgaria to Turkey, "Turkey still doesn't want people of your sort."

At the heart of Eden's refusal to call for the rescue of Jews was perhaps the Anglo-American fear that the warning would accomplish its goal and Jews would be saved—and then where would they all go? While more than 400,000 Jews of Hungary were being transported to Auschwitz and exterminated in death factories, more than 2,700 American and British planes flew over Auschwitz and successfully bombed German military facilities in the area but were never ordered to halt the trains transporting the Jews.

Yossi and his friends labored in this dark, destructive world of betrayal and shattered illusions. Yossi was, and remained throughout his life, a man of the field. Above thoughts of fame and career, he worked quietly and with mounting rage for something much larger than himself and all those involved, impelled by an ever burgeoning sense of kinship with those Jews in the mountains and the transit camps, on the ships and in Cyprus—those who were, in his eyes, the true heroes of the twentieth century. Astonishingly, quite a few arrogant sabras asked the refugees whom they were rescuing questions like "How come you survived? Did you collaborate? Were you a Kapo?" They kept repeating that classic phrase "sheep led to slaughter" coined by Abba Kovner in his famous proclamation of September 1, 1943, in which he called for armed resistance, a phrase both inappropriate and damaging in the mouths of those living in Palestine during the world war.

Chapter Six

Shaul Avigur—the man of mystery known as "the conduit of courage" in the struggle—asked Yossi to go to Greece and help bring these people on the *Knesset Israel*.

And so Yossi went. He reached a ravaged and bombed Europe, a Europe of wandering refugees, some of whom managed to return to their original locales. Flocks of refugees fought each other like creatures in the wild. Children and old people infiltrated borders, tricking the authorities, tricking each other.

Not every Palestine Jew who undertook these difficult missions grasped what Yossi grasped when they beheld orphans looking like a pack of jackals that sold, bought, and stole. Graduates of Auschwitz, Bergen-Belsen, Treblinka, they didn't learn how to be nice.

Joshua M., who would load coal on the *Knesset Israel*, had fled to the forest after his father set himself on fire at home, joining three other children who dug a hiding place for themselves. They stole food in a small town nearby and waited for the partisans to take them in. They made shoes out of birch bark and gathered mushrooms. They walked the woods for a whole year. They stole food from the pigs, since pigs were fed bran and were hated by the non-Jews in the neighboring villages. When the partisans discovered them, they sweet-talked them but refused to accept them on the grounds they were too young and handed them over to the Germans. Two of his friends were hanged on a tree before his very eyes.

Joshua M. was lucky enough to be rescued by a farmer who found him hiding. He worked for him, and then later he worked in a sort of sewing sweatshop in a labor camp for non-Jewish inmates. He found a caravan of Jews from the Caucasus who had been prisoners of war in Germany but had managed to escape. Along with them, he crossed the snowy mountains en route to Italy, and from there they went to Yugoslavia, to the *Knesset Israel*, and made their way, finally, to Palestine.

As it turned out, they would not reach Palestine on this journey; the ship would be forced to reroute to Cyprus. Eventually he reached Haifa, but once there, before he could see a house, or store, or kiosk, he was mobilized. The first place he saw was an army barracks. He had to deposit all the possessions he had amassed as means of livelihood—rings, cigarettes, condoms. They put him on a truck loaded with provisions that set out on Saturday. The first shots he fired as an Israeli were against religious Jews shouting at them, "*Shabbos! Shabbos!*" Afterward, he fought in Nebi Yosha and took part in the taking of Jaffa. He lacked an education, but since he knew something about shoes from his days in the woods, he became a cobbler in a small village in the center of the country.

Here is the chronicle of Isaac, a man whose fate was never the subject of research, who did not make it into the history books, history hardly being interested in such particulars. Isaac immigrated to Palestine on the *Knesset Israel;* years later none of his neighbors on the *moshav* had any understanding of why he enclosed his small garden with barbed wire.

Isaac, also known as Yatsek, was a short, bright-eyed man with spiky hair that turned white in the days of his youth, who managed to escape Mauthausen. During his wanderings in the woods he ate little but experienced much. When he found an angry woman there, wrapped for warmth in a burned curtain that once covered the ark in a synagogue, he felt as if he were betraying his dead father, who had been deeply religious. The woman had already lost a son in a selection. In defiance, in semirevenge against fate, she conceived in the middle of the woods and bore him a daughter. The child was shot by a Polish partisan whom they had asked for help. Somehow they managed to escape, but the woman died from exhaustion. Yatsek kept wandering, reached the port of Backa in Yugoslavia, boarded the *Knesset Israel,* and helped Yossi stage a children's play incorporating Palestine songs and declamations he had never heard before.

He sailed the pathetic ship of the dead, got captured by His Majesty's Royal Navy, suffered all their abuses, and was deported wounded to Cyprus. Six months later he left Cyprus with a certificate. But on the *Knesset Israel* he had found Malka, a girlhood friend of the woman who had been his wife in the woods. Malka had lost a daughter, too, and a husband. They married quietly, claiming that two could live even cheaper than one. Perhaps they married for love as well, but she said love was a word just for the rich. A son was born to them.

Yatsek worked for Tnuva, the dairy company, and accumulated some savings. They treated their child with kid gloves. But the boy—the sabra—was mobilized for army service on the eve of the Six-Day War. The morning after his son was called up, Yatsek went to the beach for a swim, wearing a wristwatch. The next day his wife discovered a letter: "Dearest, all my children have died. When everybody aboard the ship got sick, Amnon shouted on the megaphone, 'Sickness is forbidden!' So now tell our child it is absolutely out of the question he die in war! Water the garden. Don't dismantle the barbed-wire fence. The enemy could come at any moment. My son, it's exactly five o'clock in the afternoon. You are all that's left now."

In a situation in which the gates of countries like Australia—today remembered as safe havens for refugees—were hermetically sealed, most Jews wanted to leave Europe. It wasn't easy to live in the DP camps for an unlimited period of time. Of course, some stayed. There were even those who remained in Germany. In the early fifties, when massive immigration caused economic crisis and austerity in Israel, some feared hunger and other hardships and preferred to wait and immigrate later to countries that might agree to open their gates, but the majority truly wanted to leave. However, without the brazen adventurousness and rule-breaking audacity of those who delivered the refugees from the Valley of Death, it is doubtful the illegal immigration operation would ever have succeeded.

The entire Aliyah Beth with its more than one hundred thousand refugees, and the Aliyah after the establishment of the state with its hundreds of thousands of refugees, and every arms acquisition and flight operation with its hundreds of thousands of Jews wandering across Europe, was accomplished by about one hundred and fifty Jews from Palestine, a few dozen volunteers from America, and several from Spain. That's all. What Orde Wingate taught in the mountains of Galilee and on the Lebanese border applied here—sometimes the notion that timing is everything is a great folly.

Chapter Seven

Yossi had been serving as Professor Chaim Weizmann's military adjutant and chief bodyguard, as well as his channel of communication with the Haganah. All this he relinquished when he left the country at the request of Shaul Avigur. He had neither a passport nor any papers at all as he dodged the waves off Haifa in a small boat. Beyond the breakwater, on the open sea, he was picked up by a freighter hired to take him and the gold he carried. The captain was a Palestine Jew, a veteran seaman. The mechanic, the sailor, and the sailor's son who assisted him, were Arabs. They didn't ask questions. The captain explained that over the years one learned from the fish how to be deaf and dumb.

They entered Famagusta, the port of Cyprus, to load provisions needed to camouflage the reason for their entry into Piraeus. In a conversation with a local, he learned that Jews were to be brought to camps currently under construction on the island. Yossi listened carefully, all his senses alert. Although the Cypriot himself was not aware of the full import of what he was saying, Yossi was. He tried to draw additional details from a dealer in building materials. The man grew suspicious and did not volunteer much information, mumbling something about the British starting to construct a large detention camp for Jewish refugees on the island. It became clear to Yossi that in addition to Atlit and certain locales in Africa, Cyprus would soon serve as a site for refugee detention camps; this lent an additional urgency to the task at hand. The Jewish captain recommended they purchase oxygen tanks. Yossi bought out the entire inventory, thirty in all, but it still wouldn't be enough; one wouldn't hire a freighter just to transport thirty tanks of oxygen. Then he remembered what the Arabs in Jerusalem called *khafaf,* a lightweight pumice stone they quarried from the shores of Jaffa. That was the perfect solution. They stacked the ship with bags of gravel and set out for Piraeus. At the last moment a young Greek officer turned to them and asked if he could come along to Piraeus. Yossi gladly consented. It seemed to him that having a Greek officer aboard could only improve their cover story. At night the officer drank and babbled about the sea being full of Jews who were a more profitable catch, when sold to the British, than a cargo of plain fish.

When they left Cyprus, the sea turned turbulent. Yossi sat on the bow of the ship and watched pods of dolphins accompany them on either side. Their cruising speed was faster than the ship's. They looked lovely and evasive. Thinking about what the Greek officer had said, Yossi prayed he would be the one to catch the fish so the British would go hungry.

Upon arriving at Dodecanese, they had to navigate through all twelve islands on a very rough sea, perilously close to shore. The ship hit a sandbank and almost split apart. They were forced to stay on the island for a few days, but that gave them a chance to load fresh provisions. Thus, instead of four days as planned, it took them three weeks to reach Piraeus. During all that time they had no contact with Palestine or with any agents of Mossad le-Aliyah Beth in Greece. Nobody knew what happened to them. On the tugboat escorting them into Piraeus was somebody who called himself Yorgo, Captain Yorgo. He made all the necessary arrangements with the customs officials. Yorgo looked worried when he saw the Greek officer, until the man said he needed help and *this* Italian—pointing at Yossi—helped him. Yorgo unloaded the two suitcases filled with gold and left the tobacco boxes full of gold sovereigns with Yossi for the time being.

Captain Yorgo, the Mossad le-Aliyah Beth agent, was not much of a talker. He seated Yossi at a café in an unfinished, rather dreary building, and asked him to wait there. At one point the two boxes placed on the table were accidentally knocked over by a clumsy waiter. The sovereigns scattered across the café floor, and as if every day of his life he dropped boxes full of gold, Yossi went down on all fours and gathered the coins one by one. The people all around him sat in silence, in dark shadows. No one rose. In a poor town, after the war, gold seemed so illogical that nobody was interested. Yorgo came back and led Yossi to the Aliyah Beth headquarters.

In a dingy room covered with old, faded wallpaper, in a house rented by the Mossad, sat Ya'ani Avidov and Benyamin Yerushalmi, heroes of Aliyah Beth. Yerushalmi was assigned to the fitting of the illegal ships. Yossi related what he had heard at Famagusta about the camp that the British were setting up. The information was immediately telegraphed to Palestine. None of them had proper identification papers, but without delay they set out to reconnoiter the territory. The giant port of Piraeus was one of the largest ship graveyards in the world. Hundreds of vessels lay at anchor there after being removed from service, looking like living skeletons. Among the half-shattered ships, it was not at all difficult to conceal the Aliyah Beth boats.

The three of them spoke very little. Avidov and Yerushalmi showed Yossi the "bargains" they acquired in exchange for the two suitcases of sovereigns. The first was *Anna-Luceta,* or *Anna* for short, made in 1892 and brought to Greece with a cargo of lumber from South America. The second, *Atina,* had sunk in 1945. Dredged from the sea, it was shrouded in rust. The salt water and silt at the bottom of the harbor had corroded its keel and eaten into its sides. At this very moment they were busy at the harbor sprucing up the ships, using the equipment that had just arrived, including lumber, screws, nails, and electric fans that had to be transported from afar.

Moysh Perlman, a British intelligence officer working for the Mossad, arrived by plane armed with forged documents and the separated parts of a transmitter that Abraham Likovsky, the wireless operator, was able to reassemble into a receiver power-ful enough to contact Paris, Tel Aviv, and beyond.

Together with Mossad agents, the Bricha men who came to help refugees at their request and never took command but focused instead on organizing them had succeeded in consolidating refugees from Hungary, Czechoslovakia, and other places like Zagreb and Belgrade.

The romance with the Italians that flourished earlier, and within whose framework quite a few illegal ships were fitted for voyage, tottered under British pressure. The Greeks also turned scared, and even the French became suspicious. The burden of unemployment concerned them much more than the trials and tribulations of Jews trying to enter, or return to, their homeland. They were not looking for trouble from the British. At that time, all the European powers were at various stages of reorganization. The Mossad le-Aliyah Beth initiated contact, albeit shaky at first, with the Communist bloc nations. The tears shed by British soldiers when they liberated the death camps and saw the scenes of horror before their very eyes were avidly exchanged for Arab oil. In order to appease the Arabs, the English tried to prevent the survivors from reaching Palestine or Britain. International peace-signing committees, over which Britain had considerable control, terrorized many countries into linking these treaties with their positions on Jewish refugees.

In turn, the Yugoslavians stood to lose a great deal if they helped the refugees, but the Soviet Union, exploiting the opportunity to gain a foothold in the struggle of Palestine against the British empire, influenced Czechoslovakia and Yugoslavia to lend a hand.

Anna, soon to be renamed *Knesset Israel* and accordingly to substantially reduce the sense of Jewish helplessness, had a volume of 1,800 tons and, despite its hoary age, appeared to the Palestine Jews no less large or lovely than the *Queen Mary*.

Yossi was supplied with a passport. The ship's documents were signed with fabricated signatures. The refugees waited in camps in Yugoslavia, accustomed now to accept as their names whatever was written on their false passports or whatever was etched on their arms.

For years they had walked on pathless paths to reach the ports on the Mediterranean Sea. But it was known by now that Mediterranean ports were closing down, so it was necessary to reach the shores of the Adriatic. Some Jews returned after the war to Poland, Latvia, Belgium. Some managed to integrate themselves, mainly in France. The atmosphere in most of the countries that had been occupied by the Nazis, from which people were transported to the camps, was hostile. Some nevertheless remained. Others returned to their native lands and waited for the day when they could immigrate to America or Australia. For non-Jewish refugees, there was a place to go back to. For most Jews, not so. Zionism became more a concrete means of finding a home than an ideology, and therein perhaps lay its secret power.

The sea was the only fresh field between the vile continent— a cemetery for Jews, a scorched earth—and a possible homeland, which in many ways was a frightening place, unknown but a chance for another life. A place whose key was within reach.

The camp in Zagreb was overcrowded, but Jews kept pouring down from the mountains. Discipline became a problem. Days passed, troubles worsened, the cold increased, and for many the situation seemed hopeless. Moreover they didn't know when they would ever leave.

From the moment he arrived in Piraeus, Yossi was forced to work without pause. The agony of the people in the camp affected those working on their behalf. The Bricha men, who were usually more in danger of arousing suspicion than other Mossad groups, working as they did in hostile territory, were able to safely accelerate their pace as well. This was due largely to the TTG, which stood for *Tilches Tizi Geschaeft* (a combination of Arabic and German that translates into "kiss-my-ass monkey business"). With the benefit of both genius and luck, the Mossad created the TTG, a sham British unit that validated the presence of the Mossad and Bricha men. Undercover Bricha men saluted fake colonels who came in and out of British military camps, knowing that their days were numbered and they would soon be discovered. Their unit was fully supplied with papers, documents, signatures. Their members wore British uniforms, rode in military vehicles, wore insignias, medals, while the British never even knew they existed. The unit helped survivors by smuggling sugar, wheat, and gasoline out of British military warehouses and selling all of it on the black market. With the money they accumulated, the Mossad le-Aliyah Beth acquired equipment and additional ships. The unit had at least forty or fifty men on a regular basis and worked for two years without getting caught.

Time was short, sleep was considered a luxury, and British detectives never stopped breathing down their necks. Benyamin Yerushalmi and Yossi became experts in an area totally new to them—overhauling ships or, more accurately in their case, creating something out of nothing. They supervised the carpenters and electricians who worked around the clock, they fixed the ventillation system, they redesigned the ship's interior structure so it could hold at least three thousand people. Among all the baggage Yossi brought along with him from Palestine, experience in repairing ships was not included. And nothing prepared him for the sight of a young girl weeping without tears, a girl he would later meet on the ship, holding an imaginary doll in her hands, plucking out its eyes, and desperately rubbing herself against the walls in order to feel something that would remind her of an embrace of love. What Yossi's baggage did contain was bananas, clementines, some chocolates, dates, and three items for "ideological fortification"—a Bible, the poems of Hannah Senesh and Nathan Alterman, and Franz Werfel's *The Forty Days of Musa Dagh*.

That poor man's *Queen Mary*, which had already celebrated its golden anniversary, was not built as a luxury liner. Even in its younger days it was a junk heap. When they calculated exactly how much space each individual would be allotted, they had to consider its condition. The decision was to allow the bare minimum: fifty centimeters of living quarters per person. Eight layers of bunks were built, and in turn, they had to provide ladders and construct passageways. It was necessary to design a ventilation system throughout the space of the ship to accommodate thousands of people, to confront the fact that the engine room would be unbearably hot and therefore a partition was necessary to let somebody remain in that hell for hours. Since the coal would spread clouds of black dust, they had to find an outlet through which the pollution could escape.

The plan that evolved from these impossible but unavoidable conditions demanded an insensitivity bordering on cruelty—there could be only a few privies on deck. It was necessary to safeguard a place for the sailors, construct a plumbing system, assign locations for the distribution of food, and, most important, set aside and vacate an area for a daily walk of about an hour for breathing fresh air. They had to install a sewage system in the small, soon-to-be overloaded ship; figure out exactly where water and food would be stored; figure out how to cycle the groups of refugees from their eight levels of cramped bunk beds in the hold of the ship to the deck, so they could breathe air, eat, use the bathrooms, and bathe; and then figure out how to bring them down again to enable others to come up with minimum friction.

To accomplish all this, they would have to calculate the number in each group that would be coming on deck and appoint monitors sufficiently reliable or persuasive who, if necessary, would shove their brethren back down to the ship's hold. At the planning stage, Benyamin and Yossi had to anticipate forming a unit of "ideologically responsible toughs," carefully selected to consolidate all the survivors from the various lands, organized toughs who could maintain order without abusing their authority. It was necessary to orchestrate and coordinate in advance all the fourteen thousand trips up and down and take into consideration the fact that if too many people were on one side they could tilt and sink the ship—180 to 200 tons of humans, plus hundreds of tons of cargo, belongings, food, water, and fuel in a ship of 1,800 tons. It was necessary to determine what would happen if someone got sick and where the person would be taken. And even though they had decided not to accept pregnant women, they knew there would be some anyway; go remove from the ship a pregnant woman who spent two years walking in the mountains, and all she had was shame and very little hope. Go remove her from the ship, and tell her she should give birth on some wharf. And where would she go, even if she wanted to?

Yossi was a stranger in town. He did not speak the language. The preparations required cooperation from local inhabitants, who were not always trustworthy, especially since the British were distributing ample bribes in order to collect ever more information. From time to time Yossi would substitute a different set of forged travel documents for himself and disappear from the eyes of the suspecting workers. In order to mislead the detectives who were trying to pinpoint exactly what was going on, he alternated between two residences owned by the Mossad le-Aliyah Beth in Athens. Occasionally, so as not to be over-conspicuous, he was sent to the cinemas, even to nightclubs with their hostesses typical to port cities—pathetic and heavily made up, a phenomenon that the puritanical Palestine Jews had simply never seen before. Rather than just have a good time, he rehearsed the plans of escape from the nightclubs where the five of them would sit over one glass of whiskey, how to jump from the back windows onto the alleys crawling with famished crooks who would do anything to survive in a city trying to pull itself together, a city whose demolished houses were heated by horse manure instead of coal, which was no longer available.

It was his task to put to work Jewish camp survivors who had become experts at all sorts of semi-illegal activities, who survived the death camps because they had engaged in forging British currency as part of the economic battle the Nazis waged against the Allies. They sat cramped, hidden in niches, near the transit camps and by the ports, and forged documents. They sat in warehouses filled with canned food hoarded and concealed for the time being, all "borrowed" from the British army. These survivors whom Yossi watched sitting and concentrating on their work granted him his first bittersweet taste of what was awaiting him.

At a meeting of the Jewish agency that later investigated the *Knesset Israel*, Giora Yoseftal called the ship "a floating old age home." As far as he and a number of other Palestine leaders were concerned, there was a "bad" Holocaust where people died or survived as refugees, and there was a "good" Holocaust—that of the ghetto fighters. Some of the arrogant sabras wondered aloud why the murdered, humiliated Jews did not fight back in fury. David Shaltiel, the future commander of Jerusalem in the War of Independence, said: "Those who survived, survived because they were egoists and probably looked out for themselves first. Them, it is forbidden to pity."

After they saw the passengers on the *Knesset Israel* scuffling during their deportation, one of the agency leaders, in amazement mingled with contempt, expressed his opinion on the sort of people coming to Palestine: "They took a shtetl, including the nursery and old age home, and put it on a ship."

Ben-Gurion, the Jewish tragedian, the lapsed Bolshevist, the Hasid without a rebbe and without a God, in whose conflicted soul were intertwined the ghetto, the desert, and dreams of a kingdom, managed to comprehend this colossal helplessness. He also realized that any true resistance had been impossible over there. He understood the split forming in the community right before his eyes and said angrily and decisively: "Let us never forget that the survivors are the plaintiffs and we are the defendants."

In his weak moments, though, he said—not without boastful arrogance—that "what occurred in Poland couldn't occur in Israel. They wouldn't kill us in the synagogues." Like many others, he found it difficult to fully fathom the magnitude of the disaster made possible by the precision of the death factories. But ultimately Ben-Gurion truly understood that the survivors presented the greatest moral claim before a world that had shut its eyes and averted its face from their destruction. And this moral claim could also be turned against the Jewry of Palestine that wanted neither to hear, see, nor comprehend the conditions enabling such a slaughter.

Like someone who had never fallen into the trap of peer pressure, and after Hanita no longer associated with his teacher Yitzhak Sadeh, who was then forming the militant Palmach, Yossi remained loyal to his biological father and to all his surrogate fathers, men of action and sobriety, and no longer yearned for the courage of combat.

He was a witness to the disbanding of FOSH, which had been established at Hanita on the ruins of the Nomads, and considered Ben-Gurion correct in his firm and uncompromising position against the possibility of founding a more socialist and extreme army. And when he himself took a stand in the ideological debate and joined Ben-Gurion, he lost Yitzhak Sadeh's patronage and was left only with Wingate. He was sensitive to these refugees because he was still a lone wolf, because their situation touched some delicate entity planted in his soul. From the first moment, he not only did not disdain the mentality of the ragged refugees, but understood their misery and loved them. At some hidden unknown moment, the sabra sixth-generation Jerusalemite, the Hanita man, one of Wingate's commandos, became a Yid, an identity that some portion of Palestine Jewry understood but could not internalize until after the trial of Eichmann.

Chapter Eight

The *Anna* and *Atina* were still not ready. Since building material was lacking, everybody got involved in the effort to improvise solutions. Then suddenly Yorgo turned up to announce that the British were on to them. The Greek crew, upon realizing the enterprise involved illegal Jews, began to make threats. Bribery proved ineffective, and it took considerable push and pull before a fresh crew was collected from far-off villages. A Greek captain named Kosta, who panicked, suddenly plucked up courage, apparently just so as to take the money and run. (An interesting historical footnote: Several years later he served in the high command of the Saudi navy in Jidda.)

After the new crew asked for a guarantee that they would be dropped off at one of the islands, the pledge was given. The Anglo-Jewish journalist John Kimchi rushed over to the hotel to report that the English had found them out and, this time, would even attempt to break the rules of the game and carry out the capture inside the port—contrary to international treaties. Yorgo, too, hurried to inform them that based on his own sources the British indeed intended to raid the ships that very night, at midnight.

Yerushalmi, Yossi, and anyone else who could move quickly packed whatever they had with them. They loaded the ships with wireless radios, faucets, lumber, nails, and screws. At nightfall they went down to the ships and at ten o'clock set sail. Benyamin Yerushalmi commanded the *Anna* and Yossi the *Atina*. The English, not anticipating that the prows of the ship were pointing toward Yugoslavia, waited for them at the exit on the eastern side.

An hour before the British confiscation order went into full force, and a bit after they had succeeded in their escape, the two ships came within sight of the Peloponnesus. Yerushalmi, who was on the *Anna*, realized that his ship, because of its dimensions, would not be able to pass through the Canal of Corinth between the Peloponnesus and mainland Greece, so he would have to swerve around and circle half the island, whereas little *Atina* could cross the canal. They agreed to separate.

After they passed through the canal, the Greek captain of the *Atina* decided to cross the Aegean Sea only at night, and not out in the open sea but close to the rocky sloping shoreline studded with islands. He was afraid of Yossi's response and to some extent even acknowledged he was unfamiliar with the route he had selected. He feared going astray and landing in Communist Yugoslavia and, more than that, feared sailing along the coast of Albania, since an earlier incident had taken place there between the Albanians and the British navy. It required a great dose of persuasion and a rather undiplomatic political pep talk to keep him sailing.

After three days they reached the island of Cephalonia. The crew members, through their representatives, proclaimed that they would not proceed any further until they received the cash they had been promised. Yossi refused. Without any other choice, and fearful of losing their payment if they did not agree to continue, they consented to sail as far as Split, Yugoslavia. The distance between the two ships increased continually. The ancient *Atina* sailed slowly, and having already circumvented the Peloponnesus, Yerushalmi sailed full speed ahead on the *Anna* without waiting for Yossi. After Yossi confirmed that the *Atina* had indeed turned north, he went below in order to check the condition of the people in the belly of the ship. The captain exploited Yossi's absence from the pilot bridge to swing the ship 180 degrees and begin sailing south. Down below, Yossi realized what was happening and rushed up to the deck. The captain looked flustered, startled at the sight of Yossi bursting onto the bridge. He sputtered in his defense that there was a hitch, and they would have to return to Piraeus.

Yossi clearly knew the purpose of returning to Piraeus, where the British were waiting for them, so he instructed the members of the crew to "clarify" for the captain what he should do, and the captain then had no difficulty "comprehending" and swung around to the original direction—north. But he steered in a state of shock, making one miscalculation after another, until he finally grounded the ship on a lighthouse cliff.

The *Atina* went up the cliff, bouncing wildly until it came to a dead halt. Certain the ship had cracked, Yossi went down to investigate. The captain didn't move. One of the Greek sailors went below to assist Yossi. While they discovered no irreparable damage or any risk of sinking, the ship was definitely stuck. The captain did not look overly disappointed. On the wireless Yossi warned Yorgo, who hastened to reach them from Piraeus. With the aid of a tugboat that Yorgo had brought along with him, they very carefully pulled the *Atina* off the cliff and resumed their voyage.

They sailed past the entire coast of Albania toward Split, the largest Yugoslavian port in the Adriatic Sea. To prepare for any problem that might arise, Yossi had taught himself as much as he could about the operation of a ship. He descended to the engine room, spent hours with the crew (which would prove invaluable in the drama that would ensue aboard the *Knesset Israel*), and discussed the smallest details having to do with loading cargo, relaying water buckets, stoking coal, interpreting and regulating the temperature of the motors, the quantities of coal necessary for propulsion, cooling the furnaces, and anything else that seemed useful. By now he had already realized that the time might also come when he would have to know things that captains know, the men whose accumulated experience went far beyond swimming lessons in the Kinneret or a sailing course at the mouth of the Yarkon River.

Upon arriving at Split ahead of the other ship, Benyamin Yerushalmi moored the *Anna* at a little fishing harbor named Bačka, in a hidden inlet among the islands, and waited for the *Atina*, which was still sailing up the rocky coast in order to unite with the *Anna*. A village with small, red-roofed houses and cobblestone plazas, Bačka was a godforsaken port. It was possible to work there without fear of British spies or Yugoslavian informers, a quiet spot where they could finish fitting the boats. Despite its size, the port had waters deep enough for the ships to anchor by the pier.

When Yossi finally met up with Yerushalmi, disembarking at Split, the two drove an old car across the mountain peaks overlooking the Adriatic Sea. It was a spectacular sight that aroused some misgivings—a steep, sad, rocky, wild landscape, marking the end of the woodlands on one side and revealing a barren waste of gray, glacierlike basalt on the other. Viewing the landscape that the refugees would have to traverse to get here, Yossi envisioned the Jerusalem of his roots—the inhabited city met by a vast desert.

A strong wind swept over the valleys. It pained him to think about the refugees who at this very hour were dragging themselves and their belongings through unmarked paths, plodding single file one after another, crossing borders with the aid of smugglers or escorted by emissaries from Palestine.

In Bačka they were to be received by Sheyke Dan. Sheyke, whom Yossi loved and admired unstintingly until the day Sheyke died, was a shadowy figure and one of the legendary agents of the illegal immigration to Palestine. This virtuoso of few words, called "Lightning" because he always preferred to send telegrams, now became the Aliyah Beth contact with Yugoslavian, Romanian, and Bulgarian authorities. In the Second World War he had parachuted behind enemy lines, and unlike most of the paratroopers from Palestine who risked their lives dropping into the unknown, he had not been captured. Intuitively knowing how to blend in, he linked up with the partisans. Sheyke Dan was a righteous man, modest, witty, and in some ways innocent.

The *Anna* was being overhauled to absorb the three thousand refugees, but there was insufficient construction material in Yugoslavia. Thus, in addition to what they had brought along to Greece, they also had to import supplies from distant places. The Palestine Jews assigned to the Bricha project went around in uniforms decorated with insignias and medals purchased in a Marseilles market. And with forged documents in their pockets, they went off to secure building and installation supplies. Based on the ship's appearance, Sheyke insisted on boarding four thousand people, contrary to the majority opinion that it was much too risky. It was decided that each refugee would be permitted to take along personal belongings weighing no more than twenty-five kilos. They began working on the final details so as to board everyone as quickly as possible. Sheyke appointed Yerushalmi commander of the *Anna,* which would later be called *Knesset Israel,* and assigned Yossi his assistant, responsible for the refugees. Yoash Tsidon was designated radio operator. The Greek crew numbered eighteen sailors, most of them members of the same family.

Alongside the *Anna* anchored the *Atina,* which had a volume of six hundred tons. After a more thorough inspection of its hull, which had gotten banged up by the lighthouse cliff, they concluded that it would not be prudent to use the ship at all. It had lost its anchors, and the damage was apparently more extensive than initially estimated. Luckily another Mossad le-Aliyah Beth ship reached Bačka at that very time, the *Nisnit,* originally named *Agia Anastasia* and nicknamed by the Mossad *The Saintly One.*

The *Nisnit,* which was no less fragile than the *Atina,* was found more seaworthy. Sheyke calmed down when it became clear to him that at least 800 refugees could board it; between the two ships, 3,800 refugees would make the voyage. According to the plan, the *Anna* and *The Saintly One* would sail in tandem to the shores of Palestine at a reasonable distance from one another, and as soon as they got close enough to land, the refugees on the *The Saintly One* would be transfered to the *Anna*, allowing *The Saintly One*, the smaller ship, to slip away from the British and return to Yugoslavia to fetch more Jews languishing in transit camps already hit by winter.

The sight of the dilapidated ships anchored side by side, a scarred, small, but still Jewish navy, aroused deep emotion. It was the first time three "Jewish" ships had converged in one port. What it took in order to dream, organize, and implement this illegal immigration project, the most thrilling enterprise in the entire saga of the Zionist movement, was the arrogance of the Palestine Israelis, who always said: "Not to worry." A knack for improvisation was necessary to transport thousands of people on ships that were substandard at best and still expect things to go well. But the Mossad men, and the Palmachniks, were saturated with the sense that they had no other choice. Jews were pouring by the thousands from all over Europe in a nonstop flood, and without that Palestine Jewish arrogance, it is doubtful that the Aliyah Beth and the complicated, comprehensive Bricha operation on behalf of the Jewish refugees in Europe would ever have been realized.

To expedite the work under the growing time pressure, the Yugoslavians donated forty German prisoners of war whom they brought—by a quirk of fate—dressed in prisoners' garb. The Germans were petrified, afraid of their own shadows. But nobody was interested in harming them, there was no time for revenge, and they worked energetically and proficiently, with characteristic German efficiency. The ships, brimful with Jews, were the ultimate revenge: these former Nazi soldiers were now helping to fit the ships destined to rescue the very people they and their comrades hadn't managed to exterminate.

Yossi went out with the Bricha men to retrieve a group of refugees who had tramped from Austria to Italy through the mountains. He noticed that in the absence of family they had formed quasi communes. Young people who, after the war, found not a single member of their families alive grabbed on to each other. He saw they wanted to laugh, to live, but having forgotten how, their laughter was more like weeping. They forced themselves to sing, dance a hora, imitate the Palestine Jews. They wept and sang.

In such an encampment, awaiting the ships and meeting fellow passengers for the sea voyage ahead, these wanderers realized that they were still Jews and should unite, rally together; find shoes for the footsteps they left behind. Yossi's heart soared, for what he was participating in amounted to, as he put it without embarrassment, "the redemption of the Jewish people."

Thousands of Jews had congregated in camps near Zagreb for two months. Dollar speculators snuck in and out, risking arrest and putting the entire operation in danger. These were people who, during the two or three years since their liberation, had survived by ruses and petty scams, buying and selling cigarettes, watches, diamonds, and gold, and were now bitter and angry, unable to trust the far too clean and innocent folk from sunny Palestine with their sentimental songs, slogans, parades, and ideology.

For the five thousand wretches consumed by cold and filth who waited in camps around Belgrade, blankets sent by the Joint Distribution Committee of Canada were distributed with emotional, if somewhat dramatic, civility—one thousand blankets for five thousand men, women, children, and elderly. Some of the youngsters who boarded the *Anna* had been discovered earlier in various hiding places. One woman said, "When I look at us, the question gnaws at me, Who the hell will ever want us?"

Thus, because of their distress and their need to unite, "families" emerged that wandered together in order to survive. After they united and temporarily erased their nightmares, a modest joy was born. Perhaps there was still hope, despite everything, that they actually had somewhere to go. Perhaps their past had a certain future.

With the beginning of winter, one of the worst in years, it was necessary to come up with a larger transit camp because the fitting of the *Anna* and *The Saintly One* was taking longer than expected. Therefore they leased an unfinished edifice of Maximir University outside Zagreb, an abandoned building that did not arouse the suspicion of the British agents masquerading as librarians at the cultural center in Zagreb.

The British began sending back to Palestine the Jewish soldiers who served in the Jewish Brigade, so as to prevent them from assisting the refugees. In Yugoslavia the rescue operation worked under extremely austere conditions. A mere seventy members of Palmach, along with thirty agents of the Mossad le-Aliyah Beth and soldiers from the Jewish Brigade, constituted the grand total of the department engaged in transporting hundreds of thousands of human beings through secret channels. No leader, no military commander of the greatest stature in the world, could have transported an entire people through paths that were not paths, across the unknown, with such a handful of men to help. The only explanation is, people simply wanted to come. The Jews from Palestine were nothing more than facilitators. Jews streaming to the shores were desperate to get there. Some remained behind because there was not enough room for them, and they found other means of escape in the early 1950s. But the lion's share poured forth. Even if the Jews from Palestine had not been there to help them, Jews would have come to the shores and waited. In the years 1934 to 1945, there were those who acquired ramshackle ships on their own, some of which sank en route. Other Jews were swindled by merchants and betrayed by profiteers. Nonetheless they did not stop coming.

Sheyke Dan arrived at the camp accompanied by the former commander of the Yugoslavian partisans, who after the war had become a high-ranking official. Scanning the enormous camp as it went about its business in the bitter winter, they were struck by the women laundering their clothes in cold water, the bread-lines, the shame and sorrow. The Yugoslav conceded that it was time for him to hand over the flag of the Yugoslavian partisans to the Jewish partisans.

The food supplies, collected one way or another from American army surplus or from combat K-rations, were distributed meticulously. Despite both the inhuman conditions and the absolute determination of the people to reach Palestine, the prospect of departure was met with a significant measure of sadness. Europe had been the cradle of Jewish culture. For two thousand years they had lived there. The hatred in their hearts for the continent that slaughtered them for so many years was mixed with love.

Even in Bačka it was hard to locate trained professionals to finish fitting the ships for voyage. Winter's biting cold prevailed, and the rains kept falling. By November they had no choice but to transfer the elderly to a former German camp that the Yugoslavs allowed them to use temporarily.

While there was still time, trucks covered in tarpaulin for camouflage were brought in by Palestine Jews of the Jewish Brigade and the TTG. One freezing winter day the designated time for departure arrived. The refugees assembled in exemplary order, boarded the trucks, and left in convoys. It was a long, gloomy night, and at the spot selected beforehand, at a forsaken spot in the mountains, in a barren landscape, people were taken off the trucks and put on three rented trains, each with forty passenger cars and one dining car. The refugees were transported to a small station. A timetable had to be devised for each train's departure and expected time of arrival according to the strength of the locomotives. One Palestine Jew was assigned to each train as escort, in case of any unforeseen problem.

The passenger cars in one of the trains were partially open, and the children competed with the more experienced adults for shelter from the cold. One of them, Mitka K., who was ten years old when placed on the last train hastily leaving Auschwitz for

Buchenwald, considered himself an expert in journeys of this sort. This was his second trip on a train. He related how the Germans, alarmed by the advance of the Soviet army, emptied Auschwitz in a panic and tossed him and another thousand people into open flatbed trains on which the older inmates, weakened by their suffering in the camp, stood together tied with chains. The German soldiers, also smarting from the cold, whipped them in order to stay warm. It had been truly frigid. People were forced to stand since there was no place to sit, and they began to freeze to death while being whipped, still attached to one another.

Mitka had gone over to the embracing group and slipped in between them. That is how he arrived at Buchenwald, with all the people around him already dead. He survived thanks to the small amount of warmth exuded from them before their deaths, and thanks to the wall they formed around him. He tried to explain in his own words, perhaps to himself, that it was uncertain if they even knew he was there. "But I was a child, and I deserved to live. They died trying to protect me. And maybe they had lived long enough already."

When they entered Buchenwald, the Germans set the dogs on them. Mitka K. fled into the woods and reached Weimar one day before it was liberated. Afterward, he wandered through a devastated Germany. Nobody wanted to take in a filthy child. He killed a dog that bit him, but when a wounded dove he had found died in his hands, he buried it and really wept for the first time since his hardships had begun. He formed a mound of earth for a marker in its memory, decorated it with dry leaves, and on the piece of paper that he attached to one leaf, he wrote the name of his dead mother.

Jewish soldiers from the American army found him roaming around near Munich—he couldn't remember how he got there. And now he was in an open train traveling to the ship *Anna*, showing other children how to stay warm among people who were freezing but not dead this time, traveling not to death in Buchenwald, but to life in the land of Israel.

With blue lips and voices that were barely audible, they tried to be happy and sing, "*Hine mahtov umanayim, shevet achim gam yachad . . .*" ("How good and how pleasant for brothers to sit together . . ."). "What kind of pleasantness," said Mitka, "what sort of togetherness can exist when we have no mouths!" And he laughed the laugh of a boy who had learned how to live from the dead whose belongings he had rifled to discover a hidden ring here and there, which he would sell to the SS men who would not have let him live if not for the rings and diamonds he found on the dead. That was how he had purchased another week, another two weeks, of life in the camps, until he was liberated. What good was it to "sit together as brothers"? They traveled to the port with blue-and-white flags fluttering from the windows in the cold wind. These people who had outwitted the French, Italian, English, Austrian, and Czech police, even the American MPs, were now seated in crowded train cars or jammed in open flatbeds, hoping their hardships would cease.

After a journey of considerable duration from the camps outside Zagreb, the freight trains descended and meandered their way toward Bačka. In accordance with the initial plan, the ships had enough provisions for a journey of six to seven days. Now it was clear that the voyage would take much longer, so the plan had to be readjusted to twenty-three days. The *Anna* alone needed 90 tons of food—4 tons of provisions per day. The food for each person included 350 grams of bread, 100 grams of jam, 150 grams of fish or meat, both canned, 80 grams of cheese, and, for a treat, 1 onion per person. The moldy bread would merely supplement the dry onion.

They could not find appropriate baby food. Now and again Yossi managed to turn up with a clementine or an apple, but to most of the infants he could not be of assistance. By chance he located a limited supply of apples in one of the storerooms, which he allocated to the sick and the pregnant women. Whatever was left over was distributed to the children and the most elderly. The bread that they bought in Bačka, though baked according to a German recipe devised specifically for soldiers of the Wehrmacht to keep their bread fresh for fifty days, was moldy from all the moisture. The children were issued a supplement of what came to be called "penicillin," bread shrouded in green.

Later Yossi said that trying to explain their overwhelming eagerness to board the ship was like trying to account for the sun, the air, and fresh bread. Hundreds of thousands of people who at moments of breakdown asked, "Why did this happen? Why to us in particular? Where was God? And where is the eternity of Israel?" knew there was no answer. One woman said, "I saw Palestine soldiers of the Jewish Brigade. At first I was glad. I touched their insignias written in Hebrew. I was excited to see a Star of David on their uniforms, as if we were already in our homeland. But then I got angry with them. Big-shot heroes, where were you till now?"

Chapter Nine

On November 2, the anniversary of the Balfour Declaration, the trains came in sight of the ships at timed intervals one after another, as scheduled beforehand. The last train was late and arrived without its dining car, so they had to reduce the food rations even more. Flags were waved and whistles blown in celebration; the fanfare was spirited and unrestrained. Yossi was a full partner in this typical Palestine Jewish attempt to celebrate everything with the pathos of declamation and ceremony. At twenty-seven Yossi was bringing to Palestine more than three thousand people whose shame and anger he was just then discovering. Facing a sea of blue numbers, witnesses to the sacrifice served on blue iron trays, Yossi organized a festive assembly similar to the ones held in the Palestine youth movements, which were always an effort at rising above the wasteland of Palestine, the dust, the heat waves.

In honor of the occasion, Yossi, Benyamin Yerushalmi, and their comrades donned khaki ensembles that seemed to them at once festive and military. The refugees heard sirens, and blue-and-white flags were raised and lowered. "Hatikva" was sung over and over. As they neared the ships that looked like holding pens, despite the cold they rolled up their sleeves consisting of four or five layers of clothing that made them sweat. The brightened blue numbers glowed in the pale gray light. For the moment each of them was a number, not a person. Yossi was devastated. They saw how distraught he was, and someone laughed: "Number 14,667, that's me! *Dos iz mir!*"

In perfect order they boarded the ships in groups of thirty-five. The *Anna* set sail first, and *The Saintly One* followed in its wake. The night stretched as if it would last forever. The next morning Yerushalmi, Yossi, and the rest of the team officially introduced themselves to the refugees through a megaphone, in Hebrew. The refugees remained silent. Someone translated what was said into Yiddish, then into Romanian, and then Hungarian as well. The general feeling was that a chapter had ended, but also that something obscure, something that hadn't quite manifested itself yet, had begun. The winter weather got even colder, and there wasn't enough water. Washing or laundering in hot water was out of the question. Yossi went down to the storage area. The children, most of whom were orphans, had gathered in the corners as soon as they saw the thirty centimeters allotted to each of them and begun to play with buttons and balls made of crumpled paper. The refugees didn't trust anybody and wore all the clothing they had. The heat, mingled with their sweat, became unbearable. When Yossi announced on the loudspeaker that food would be distributed only in a clean and orderly environment, the hint was taken and they began to look after themselves.

The sailors were forced to vacate their cabins in the stern of the ship to make room for a temporary infirmary, which housed eleven pregnant women. Despite the explicit instructions to the contrary, they had decided to embark these women. Some had lost children in the war, some had remarried. Others had become pregnant in hopes of memorializing their dead. And there were those who wore crosses around their necks and said they would never want to bear Jewish children because they would only get put in ovens. Young women with repressed rage in their eyes would lift their hands to the skies and scream in horrible pain, "You are human beings! We are numbers; numbers don't bear children that then become human beings. Numbers breed numbers, and there is no need for any more numbers."

Yossi summoned the representatives of the political parties and the youth movements and confirmed that a ship's council would be selected, headed by Yitzhak Artzi, and he made sure that the grounds for membership in the council would be acceptable to everybody. Leaders were picked and tasks assigned. It was critical that everything work like a Swiss watch despite the wretched conditions, otherwise there would be chaos. Each group was to receive food and water three times a day, and porters would work in shifts to lower buckets of water to the storerooms below. Rounds of sanitation duty were set up.

In the labyrinth of eight decks, notwithstanding the advance planning, confusion began to reign. The demand upon the refugees to maintain model discipline was met with instinctive opposition. After all, in the past ten years order had been the enemy. Yossi and Yerushalmi were intent on extinguishing the flames of frenzy that flared up again, and it took prodigious effort to get the refugees to adjust to the new quasi concentration camp they themselves had selected, this time of their own free will.

There were some who suddenly didn't want to go on or were unable to. They gave up and lay half-dead, awaiting the end. Depleted and dejected, they would not come up on deck to eat or even use the privies. Still, each person clung to his or her own tiny quarters. There was thirst for space and separation on the floating village. Each fifty-centimeter area was sealed off with sheets and paper—a symbolic attempt at privacy. Yossi organized groups of youths to assist the elderly up and down the stairs to their steerage quarters. The bugle of the bugler boy, who wore on his sleeve the tag Yossi had designed, blew nonstop in order to dye the ugly present in a future radiance, even if it might never come.

The infirmary was run by doctors who had been rounded up from the large community of refugees. They insisted on quarantining the syphilis-infected women whom Yossi had refused to put ashore in spite of the risk of spreading the disease. He hated knowing that this quarantine engendered a sense of ostracism and self-pity relative to the other passengers, the "free" ones in the huge penfold. But good intentions, he told himself again and again, did not justify stupidity. The women were not at fault.

Many of them had been raped by the Germans, and his only concern was that they receive medical treatment. In their faces he saw reproach and a sense of betrayal. They slept by themselves, and nobody dared come close to them.

At the sight of the pandemonium of thousands of people stumbling and bumping into each other, they decided to alter the course of traffic on the decks. Since the passengers kept going astray in the jumble of corridors, a set procedure for negotiating the passageways was necessary. Yossi and Yerushalmi established that everyone would always, without exception, stay to the right when ascending or descending the ladders, so traffic would circulate in a regular direction, for if each person went up and down just twice a day, the total number would come to fourteen thousand ascents and descents, which was feasible only if they went in one direction.

The overcrowding and hunger of the pregnant women was heartbreaking, and Yerushalmi and Yossi were determined to alleviate their discomfort. They decided to allot three buckets of water for the infirmary, which resounded with the cries of women in labor. Every bucketful of water lowered below was like an attempt at extinguishing the fires of hell with just one drop of water. And then the buckets would be raised immediately because of the shortage on deck, too.

After two days Yossi finally went to bed. But right after departure a storm gathered, raging and roaring like a gigantic waterfall. It was a *bora*, the storm known as the curse of the Adriatic Sea—a cyclone of sorts: a sudden gust of wind created from a warm stream of air moved rapidly across the barren basalt mountains without forests to impede its path, descended abruptly with enormous force, and, like a gigantic barrel upended all at once, released all the water it contained. The deluge filled the deep fjord and in a few minutes raised the height of the waves six or seven meters.

The two ships, pitching and rolling like walnut shells, were swept by the strong winds toward the craggy islands. The skipper on the *Anna* tried to head for the nearby village of Zada, but it was impossible to steer in the storm. Had he succeeded in doing as he wanted, the ship would have sunk. The *Anna* was forced, therefore, to drop two anchors, which accomplished nothing. The current dragged the ship along with its anchors. Yossi and Yerushalmi conferred and, during their talk with the skipper, activated the propeller. So doing, they at least managed to remain in place and forestall being swept onto the rocks.

The Saintly One, or as they called it, *The Little One*, sent a message by wireless that its motor had died and the ship was being hurtled in the torrent toward an area that had been mined in the world war. The Greek skipper on the *Anna*, finding himself at the helm of a boat that looked like a floating hearse, gave up, crossed himself, and awaited death. Yossi went below to offer words of encouragement to everyone. People vomited and asked, "Is this what all our efforts have come to?"

Anna sailed convulsively toward *The Saintly One*, and as they approached each other, *The Saintly One* reported that its motor had resuscitated. Two hours later, however, the motor shut down again, and once more they called for help. From the *Anna*, ropes were tossed to it repeatedly, but to no avail. *The Saintly One* began to drift toward the mined area, with eight hundred young refugees aboard. From the bridge of the *Anna*, Yossi and Yerushalmi watched *The Saintly One* toss in the wind, swept by the breakers.

While the waves reached the height of the masts, the *Anna* was still unable to latch on to *The Saintly One*. Their hearts went out to the eight hundred young refugees. With great difficulty Yossi moved toward the bridge as the wind blew him back. The masts were about to crack, and if they did, they would hit the deck hard. The force of the gales continued to pick up, heavy dark clouds continued to unleash short but powerful bursts—like an avalanche of rocks—from the mountain peaks to the straits below.

Suddenly the wind shifted and *The Saintly One* swerved to the right and was saved from the mines. But the turn was too sharp; the ship was swept toward the sandbank and thrown against the rocks with crushing force, and water began to pour inside.

Even as the ship smashed into the sandbank, the wind toyed with it. The ship rocked backward a few meters from the shore, only to crash into the sandbank again and again. It endured a severe beating and finally started to split apart. Instinct guided the passengers. With each impact they threw themselves overboard onto the rocks. Not one of them drowned. Yossi feared that the youngsters would be too bold and get crushed between the sinking ship and the rocks. But they were schooled in the rules of survival and knew how to get out from under. Only after all of them had abandoned ship did it shatter completely. Yossi watched from afar as they reached safety and then calmly, without panic, sat on the rocks, completely exposed, while the deluge continued to assault them. There they sat, waiting quietly.

The skipper on the *Anna* notified Yossi and Yerushalmi that he didn't have a map of the minefield, but he knew that the area was very narrow and certain to cause trouble. Yossi felt as if his hands were tied. Sailing away from the minefield and escaping wasn't enough, because the *bora* was blowing from the east so strongly that the old mines were likely to tear loose from their anchors and rush with the current through the only outlet, right at the *Anna*.

The *Anna* was now at a halt. Again it dropped its anchors while Yerushalmi and Yossi tried to figure out some way to reach the youngsters trapped on the rocks. A passing fishing boat alerted a Yugoslavian warship in the immediate vicinity. Yerushalmi came on deck and requested point-blank, in his rough but authoritative style, that they approach the island and offer relief. The Yugoslavian captain treated the request as an order and sailed off toward the island. The "island" was nothing but a huge projecting boulder shrouded in a mist of waves and rain. *The Saintly One*, battered by its contact with the rocks in the heavy wind, began to sink. But while there was still time, Yerushalmi tried to unload as many provisions as possible.

The rain became a flood. All at once, darkness descended. Through the long night the crew picked out the survivors and raised them to the Yugoslavian warship. They sat in groups on the deck, wrapped in blankets, attached to each other to keep warm.

At the break of dawn Yossi and Yerushalmi counted them with gathering relief: all eight hundred refugees were rescued.

The Yugoslavian warship escorted the *Anna* to a small village named Sibnik not far from Split. Sheyke Dan was alerted, and he launched a vigorous operation to assist the *Anna* and the survivors.

The only option was to quickly construct additional quarters on the *Anna*. Working steadfastly around the clock, they spanned the deck with a wooden awning covered in tarpaulin, in order to increase the number of sleeping quarters shielded from the weather and from anticipated British airplanes. In turn, they had to pack people below deck even tighter. The eight hundred youths were divided into two groups: half were brought below, and half were housed on the deck.

Meanwhile, four out of the six days of the planned passage had already elapsed. The moldy bread that the children couldn't chew anymore was tossed into the sea. Yossi and Yerushalmi went ashore and, with the help of a Yugoslavian official, organized a massive campaign to bring clothing to the survivors and provisions to the ship. And in another operation, so fantastic it might have been concocted for Hollywood, the entire village of Sibnik was asked to bake bread. Thousands of loaves were baked throughout the night in bakeries, houses, restaurants, and little farms near the village. Essentially, the inhabitants of Sibnik sacrificed their own bread, donating the equivalent of what the village consumed in a whole week. The refugees disembarked, formed a line a few hundred meters long, then passed from hand to hand the bread, coal, warm clothing, and other items, all the way to the ship's storerooms.

In the process, one of the female passengers had an appendix attack and was lowered to the shore with a crane, together with her bowed and weeping husband. At exactly the same time, it was reported that a child was born in the delivery room, so even as they lost two they gained one. At this point the total number of passengers was 3,847: 1,905 men, 1,487 women, and 455 children, and by the end of the voyage another 10 were added, born after they had set sail.

The *Anna* again headed out to sea at slow speed. They passed the entire length of the Yugoslavian border, hugging the shore in fear of mines. But as soon as they left the Adriatic and entered the Mediterranean a storm hit, and they could no longer control the ship.

That same day, as the sea struck and slapped, the second child was born. In the storm a heavy door tore loose, fell, and crushed him. The sight of the dead child shook Yossi to a degree that amazed him in light of all he had already seen: the injustice of such an innocent, dying like this after Auschwitz. He summoned one of the rabbis and asked him to organize the burial. To his amazement, the rabbi insisted that the child would have to be circumcised first. Yossi decided not to object. In order to circumcise the child, they had to give him a name. The mother couldn't talk. The father was shattered, in absolute despair. They all stood around the sobbing mother, who lay on the table that vibrated in the stern of the antiquated ship. At the woman's bedside, an argument erupted when another rabbi came and claimed that according to the law, prayer was unnecessary since the child never achieved the status of a *bar kiumah*, a live creature, and therefore circumcision was not required. The controversy sickened Yossi; he had never imagined that the first death aboard ship would be an infant. They finally decided to bury the child at sea.

They waited until nightfall, because in the light of day the burial would have been unbearable. They took an empty crate of canned goods, cleaned it, placed the infant inside, and locked it. The father, a religious man, could not restrain himself from saying kaddish, the prayer for the dead. All wept. Yossi wrapped the crate in the national flag and tied it with the chain of the anchor, and when a third rabbi came and explained that a eulogy was unnecessary, Yossi assumed control over a burial ceremony almost devoid of ritual. Below deck, the mother lay sobbing bitterly. The father stood trembling. It was already midnight. At Yossi's request the captain attended the ceremony in uniform, and Yossi was more shaken than he had been in years. Something about this moment frightened him and brought all his self-doubt to the surface—"Who am I? What authority do I have?" He pulled himself together, waited for a rising wave, then in perfect silence saluted and instructed two sailors to slide the infant to the sea along a plank extending from the deck.

The weather began to improve. They resumed sailing and approached the Peloponnesus. In the maze of small islands before the peninsula, another storm broke, rocking the ship with its force. They quickly reduced their speed to four knots. The wind and waves began to sweep the ship toward the shore. The skipper and the sailors were in shock. There was nothing the skipper and crew could do to control the course of the ship. Yossi stood on the pilot deck, thinking, In a few moments the ship will crash against the shore and split like *The Saintly One*, and its decks and its hold carry not just teenagers, but the elderly, the sick, pregnant women, children. On the deck stood the four hundred youths, housed there after the sinking of *The Saintly One*, who once again saw their ship running amok, completely helpless against the power of the elements.

Yossi knew there were not enough lifeboats to save four thousand people, not even four hundred. He knew there were no life belts. He knew that most of the people were not able to swim. In an effort to lift their spirits, he asked the mandolin orchestra, which he had established a few days earlier, to play. The women, queasy from seasickness, scrambled on deck with difficulty, stood in the strong wind, and played. One woman collapsed in a swoon. A child was struck by the deck cable. The crane slipped, and two sailors tried in vain to stabilize it. The ship was swept straight toward the rocks like a piece of lumber in a flash flood, and at every moment the rocks loomed larger.

At sunrise they all knew the end was approaching. But as they stood bleary-eyed on the pilot deck, fettered by their impotence against the laws of nature, all of a sudden—as in an old tale of wonders, facing the Greek islands engulfed in legend, facing Sparta, whose battles, leaders, and war with Athens Yossi knew from his first visit there years before—a miracle occurred. The direction of the wind shifted abruptly, and within moments the same wind that swept them in her fury toward the Peloponnesus made a ninety-degree turn, and the ship that was just about to smash against the rocks swerved gently into a powerful current of breakers and got dragged away from the coast into the arms of the open sea. The sun was already shining. Stabilized, the ship sailed with confidence. The orchestra played. And people who, until now, had been holding their breath in terror, obeying each and every instruction given them, now burst onto the deck in an uproar. To drink water! To stand for hours on line at the latrines! To talk!

They sailed east, skirting the Peloponnesus, and the winds gradually eased.

The children who had grown up in Auschwitz and other camps got into the habit of coming on deck so they could be closer to Yossi. They began to speak. They wanted this Jewish commander from Palestine to listen. The proximity of death aboard the ship triggered memories suppressed deep inside them in a vain effort to forget. Yossi was different, foreign, not one of them. But with the instinct of survivors, they trusted him. He won the hearts of these orphans with scorched roots, who needed to test his own vulnerability, to play their tune for him, to cautiously and unhurriedly express their feelings of closeness to him. For them it was important that at least one person who had never been there should understand.

One of the children sat on the rail as darting shafts of sun flashed through the clouds, and told of how—during a liquidation of the ghetto—he saw children he knew from school electrocute themselves. Another child related in broken syllables how the skulls of an entire class of students got smashed along with their teacher, their principal, and a woman passing by on her way somewhere, how their heads were knocked against the sidewalk. How Hanka screamed, "I'm seven years old, don't kill me!" And the German laughed and forced her to kiss the corpse of her dead mother and only then strangled her. One child related how in Sernik, near the Polish city of Minsk, the Germans attacked them with rottweilers trained to kill and the Gestapo amused themselves by tossing children into the wells, and how the Hitler Jugend used Yitzhak and Mishka and some other children laced against the wall for target practice.

Now, Beethoven's violin concerto was heard on the loudspeakers. As usual, people were lining up for something: water, bread, the latrines. Yossi left the children and went to participate in a meeting of the ship's council, in which it was decided to issue a daily newspaper in four languages. The editorial board was selected, as were the members of the cultural committee. Journalists, writers, and poets benefited from scraps of information provided by the wireless operator. Whatever they didn't hear from him, they made up. In spite of the space constraint, Yossi designated a place for a "youth club." They organized classes in various subjects: poetry, Judaism, Bible, the history of Palestine,

Zionism, socialism, world history, philosophy, art. Members of the different parties held debates. Yossi found them infinitely entertaining, in that even here everyone had to feel he was correct, though the heated and ferocious ideological struggles were over parts of Palestine they had never seen.

Samuel Katz, the future newspaper caricaturist for *Al Humishmar*, drew a daily lampoon that always carried some absurd caption, such as "Today's refreshments—cookies!" or "From today on, nobody works—don't object!" Classes became more and more specialized: Leninism, Russian literature, Schopenhauer's misogyny, Dickens, Shakespeare. The debates distracted people from the resurging storms at sea and the overcrowding, and allowed them to immerse themselves in another world. They dealt with the future of the nation, Napoleon's defeat in Russia, the importance of personality in history according to Plechanov, Borochov's inverted pyramid, the teachings of Trotsky and also those of ben Yehuda, who had revived the Hebrew language.

A vote was held for the Zionist Congress taking place at that time. According to the Balfour Declaration, every Zionist was allowed to vote. So forty ballot boxes were set up on the ship, and in the middle of hell people stood in the cold, biting wind, thrilled at the prospect of exercising their right to an opinion.

The Greek crew had indicated earlier that they wouldn't sail to the shores of Palestine. A rendezvous was arranged for them to be picked up at the island of Camellia Nissi by a trawler. Benyamin Yerushalmi had to disembark as well. Assigned the task of fitting an additional ship, he couldn't risk falling into the hands of the British, who had placed a high price on his head. Besides, he was the one selected to represent the ship and its refugees at the Zionist Congress.

Because he was familiar with the uninhabited, mountainous island of Camellia Nissi, Yerushalmi recommended that they anchor there. When he and Samek had brought the *Henrietta Szold* to this island, the Greeks told him that a few years earlier, in 1940, a ship named *Pancho* had arrived there, whose voyage from Bratislava had been financed by its passengers. The British had refused to allow the small ship to proceed, and it dashed to pieces against the island rocks. The captain and crew fled, and the Jews were left without food, water, or shelter. They were spotted by an Italian plane, and an Italian warship retrieved them and brought them to Rhodes. All 509 Jews were handed over to the Germans, but for some reason the Germans indicated they didn't want them. The Jews remained in Italy, and after the war all of them immigrated to Palestine.

With Yerushalmi remaining on the island, the command passed to Yossi. He assembled the crew for a meeting and listed the problems that were bound to arise in the absence of the Greek crew. The ship council said it would do whatever was required.

As they neared the island, a Mossad le-Aliyah Beth fishing boat arrived, as coordinated in advance, and collected Yerushalmi and the Greek members of the crew in order to ferry them to Piraeus. While they were disembarking, Yossi—now commander of the *Knesset Israel*—stood beside Reuben Hirsch, the navigator who was immediately appointed captain, and asked some of the crew to stay. Yossi said, "With four thousand people here, I need at least a few professional sailors." But the Greeks were afraid, and except for the second mechanic, who finally agreed and was appointed chief of the engine room, all of them refused to stay. Thus Yossi was expected not only to bring the "floating Auschwitz" to Palestine, but to train some of the passengers to sail the ship.

The training of the passengers was no small matter. After the trauma of the Holocaust, none of them was in spectacular physical shape. Still, Yossi and the more experienced Reuben did find a few boys and girls whom they were able to teach how to hold the wheel and read the compass, how to be at home in maps and maintain constant contact with the engine room, which also had to be manned by the greenest of amateurs.

The ship sailed east, close to the Turkish coast, and at a council meeting representing all the political parties an argument erupted over the system of signals they should adopt in case of capture. As if it were some surrealist play about a ship with thirteen privies for four thousand people, babies newly born on improvised delivery tables, limited and partially moldy provisions, and diminishing water supplies.

Yossi saw their task on the ship as resembling a thousand Hanitas. After war, camps, humiliation, loss, inhuman physical hardship, backbreaking journeys in the cold, in the heat, in hunger, they were proud to be fighters, not victims. This core, for Yossi, was the source from which to draw strength and motivation, but it also engendered a not so simple logistical problem. The youngsters volunteered for various missions with intense enthusiasm but no experience. They saw themselves as daring guerrilla fighters, but as one of them said, an idea could sometimes kindle a fire in dry bones, yet it took no responsibility for those who believed in it.

Of the reconstituted crew, the most remarkable was S., a young man who limped because his legs had frozen in forced labor while cutting down trees in the snow. Although he could hardly stand, he wouldn't relinquish his right to work in relaying coal from the storeroom to the engine. S. told how in a village in Yarmitch near the river Neman, the Germans concentrated the Jews, including his parents and his entire family. How they marched them into the river with gunfire and, as soon as they reached deep waters with just their heads bobbing, the Germans ordered them to come out and repeat the scene over and over, until their strength was depleted. Nobody screamed, nobody begged. The Germans instructed them to exit the water dancing because the nation of Beethoven loved music and dance. The boy went on to describe how later the Jews were shot and their bodies were then swept away by the current.

* * *

These refugees were improbable sailors. One didn't learn how to be a sailor, to work on a bridge or in an engine room, by trekking through forests for two years to the shores of Palestine, which—according to the myth proffered them—already began on the open shores of Europe. They knew of the British iron wall, but they chose not to think about it.

Electrical problems forced them to train electricians to make repairs and improvise options. The council insisted that the daily gazette continue to be written in Yiddish, Hebrew, Romanian, and Hungarian in order to keep people busy. The newspapers would be written down several times over and then delivered by the children to all corners of the ship to keep them occupied and endowed with a sense of purpose. The ship crept along. The initial calculations fizzled, as time stretched, hunger deepened, and the supply of drinking water dwindled. Despite all attempts, the ship could not increase its speed. It was necessary to avoid overtaxing the antiquated wobbling vessel, lest it sink to the depths.

It was their knack for improvisation that kept them alive and enabled them to man a ship carrying nearly four thousand people with just two professional sailors aboard. A "lost and found" was established, run by young women in shifts, so people would know how to locate what they lost, since their "property" was all they had left. The flute and mandolin orchestra continued to play on the deck and at children's gatherings. And to the children who didn't want to come out to the deck for songs or games, Yossi distributed morsels of bread if they felt dizzy. In the evening a concert was given in the stern, comprising an additional accordion, trumpet, and several violins that were previously played in one of the camps. The festive concert concluded with the Palmach anthem. Hundreds assembled on deck to listen. Yossi sent musicians to hidden corners below deck, to places where people lay gasping for breath, if only to ease their agony just a bit. And on the loudspeakers lectures could be heard on the Punic Wars, on the conquering of the Valley of Hafar in the thirties, on

Immanuel Kant, who never left the city of Königsberg, where the residents set their watches by his daily constitutionals.

Unanimously the crew decided to sail between the Turkish coast and Cyprus, so as to reach Alexandretta with maximum speed. At the wheel stood, among others, a tall strong girl who did good work. Her name was Ruth, and Yossi encouraged her to talk; he was struck by her reticence regarding whatever she did or didn't do during the war. There were certain moments when she would suddenly open up, say something, touch the numbers on her arm, laugh to herself, refusing to release the tears locked inside her, and focus totally on the wheel—a task that typically demanded considerable training, but one that came naturally to her.

One of the things that caught Yossi's attention time and time again was the way the boys stood on the ships. From habit they always tried to look taller than they were; in the camps their height had counted for everything. The short ones were sent to the gas chambers. They developed various methods to stretch themselves and appear taller, and this made Yossi's heart sink. As the girl at the wheel explained, "We're all fragments. Walking corpses."

Agnes, the sixteen-year-old girl bearing the SS tattoo, the sad girl, the lost yet brave one, would scream in her sleep at night, and Yossi, at the head of her bed, would try to calm her. He taught her the poet Rachel's lyrics. She loved to hear his voice and learned the words from his mouth. When she sang, "I have not sung you, my country, not brought glory to your name, with the great deeds of a hero or the spoils a battle yields," she became a symbol of courage for him. He may even have envied that courage, and that was perhaps what the children sensed and loved in him—that a man so strong, experienced, and mature as he could actually envy *them*.

Toward evening, by one of the derricks, Yossi saw a girl of about twelve standing facing an accordionist who was playing his instrument, for nobody in particular, except perhaps the fish. She looked at him with despairing eyes. A passerby told him the girl sang well but was shy. Meanwhile violinists came on deck. She approached them with hesitation, touched a violin, as if to catch the sound of the accordion with the vibrato of the violin, and began to sing. At that moment two night-watch groups came on deck, each group comprising one hundred people. They stood entranced. Her voice could touch hearts.

Overnight she became the little star of the ship. With Agnes she sang the song of the partisans, the one they had carried from the transit camps like food for the soul. They sang with feeling, "*Zog nit keyn mol az du geyst dem letstn veg, himln blayeneh farshteln bloye teg . . .*" ("Never say the end is near, darkest skies can always clear . . ."), and with teary eyes, as though recalling something long past, she went on to sing, "*Mayn shtetl brent . . .*" ("My shtetl is on fire . . ."), and some songs in Romanian, swaying her body while she sang, as in a dance. Hundreds of hungry, thirsty people stood there and wept. Afterward, she ran below. And the sea continued to surge.

Chapter Ten

I t was extraordinary that a ship without a crew could manage to make progress while the sea, as if out of spite, acted up so severely that the voyage took even longer than the grim forecasts that had to be revised continually throughout the journey.

When they were about to pass the coast of Turkey, Yossi realized that the moment of truth was at hand. He summoned the council for an urgent session: their water supply was almost used up, and what remained was contaminated. The furnaces were gorging on the little coal that was left. Soon they would have to feed the engines with the wood used to construct the bunk beds. Yossi served pickles and juice during the meeting, and in the process they heard a plane circling overhead.

Stooping, they ran to the deck. The two-engine plane descended, almost reaching the height of the masts. From the hideaway behind the tarpaulin, they could see the pilot signal: "Who are you?" Yossi went to the navigator deck and signaled back: "We're a freighter!" Again the pilot signaled, and Yossi replied: "We're a freighter flying the Panamanian flag, 1,800 tons, a crew of eighteen men sailing from Algiers to Alexandria, with a stopover at Alexandretta."

The plane vanished. Yossi decided not to alter their course, hoping the pilot hadn't spotted the passengers. He announced that from now on they would sail at night in pitch black and that people would be allowed to come on deck only under the cover of darkness.

In order to prepare for what was to come, those with technical abilities were asked to construct weapons from whatever was at hand. Yossi sensed that the British would not hesitate to attack. They fashioned weapons from tin cans, coal, and used oil. The anxious multitude invaded the deck in waves. In the sky, more planes appeared. Like scared mice, the refugees fled for their lives as the deck was suddenly flooded in blinding light, from all directions, exposing the crowd in flight.

A destroyer that they hadn't been able to spot earlier sailed close to them. Without the luxury of other weapons, in a quasi attack of fury and folly, people began to sing "Hatikva," and somebody was overheard proclaiming fervently, "I swear, we were united like this only in the crematoria."

The planes disappeared in the direction of the Turkish coast, and the destroyer, which found it difficult to navigate in these waters, pulled away. Yossi knew this was just a temporary lull. Improvised arms were assembled, and everyone prepared for his designated task and mission.

That night Yossi stood tense as a bowstring on the pilot bridge, forgetting everything but his search for Mt. Musa Dagh.

From afar, near the sea lane to Palestine, he discovered with the aid of binoculars Mt. Musa Dagh southeast of Antioch. Its peak was one thousand meters high and capped in perpetual snow. Suddenly he again became that Jerusalem boy who used to read aloud, together with his friend Tsvi Spector, passages from the book about the genocide of the Armenian people. For a moment he felt alone, more alone than he had felt in his whole life. Here he was, the leader of four thousand refugees who would live or die depending on his individual skill—without benefit of instructions, help, discussions, or analysis with partners in responsibility.

The Armenians who had survived the great slaughter and lived in an enclave in southern Turkey had abandoned their villages. They had refused to be driven out or murdered like their kinsmen. They had climbed—five thousand people in all—to the heights of Musa Dagh. They had dragged along with them their meager provisions, the cattle and sheep they had, and whatever household goods they could carry. The tall, barren mountain served as their natural fortification, which from its steep western side dropped straight to the sea. And on this sea, on a pilot bridge, now stood Yossi, who knew down to every detail where the paths of this tall mountain led and could distinctly see the rocky cliffs embracing the feet of the mountain, creating a sublime prodigious fortress.

He thought about Hanita, about Yitzhak Sadeh, about lost wars, about the few against the many, about his life as a fighter in a hopeless cause, and about what else he could possibly do. He focused on the mountain, rising rock by rock, stone by stone, like a colossal pyramid. On its crest thousands of Armenians had settled. Unable to reach them, the Turks encircled them with intent to kill. For Yossi, the five thousand Armenians besieged on the mountain were still present, in the form of these very refugees he was now bringing with him; after all, both groups constituted a nation or entity, even a state, for on this mountain the remnant of the Armenian nation had been saved from the genocide that had befallen its majority.

Yossi was not familiar then with what the American Armenian author William Saroyan wrote years later: "I should like to see any power of the world destroy this race, this small tribe of unimportant people, whose wars have all been fought and lost, whose structures have crumbled, literature is unread, music is unheard, and prayers are no more answered. Go ahead, destroy Armenia. See if you can do it. Send them into the desert without bread or water. Burn their homes and churches. Then, see if they will not sing and pray again. For when two of them meet any-where in the world, see if they will not create a New Armenia."

On the mountain—as Yossi-Amnon knew—there was self-defense, a command post. The Turks approached, and though they were repulsed, the situation of the besieged worsened. Their food was nearly gone. They set up a flagpole and hoisted a Red Cross flag and also waved signs toward the sea emblazoned with "Christians, help us!" Nobody came.

The Armenians made forays into nearby Kaleb to get food. They fought to the bitter end, fanatic about their right to independence in the midst of their despair.

On Musa Dagh they had formed a small state, like the refugees on the ship. They recited poetry, staged plays, held philosophical and political discussions, chose leaders. Yossi remembered with total identification that Werfel's narrative described the authority, songs, and dances of the besieged in the fortress, the small military state, brave and dying from starvation. And it all became clear to him: Here were four thousand survivors of a different disaster.

For Werfel, the forty days of Moses on Mt. Sinai served as a symbol, an analogue. Like Moses, Bagradian, the hero of the Armenian struggle, was drawn from a basket and raised in Pharaoh's palace. Like Moses, Bagradian was not a born leader but a man of soul and imagination, a rootless revolutionary without a homeland, compelled to fulfill his role because of overwhelming circumstance, transformed into a hero once he took charge on the mountain. And like Moses, he assumed total responsibility for the lives of five thousand men, women, and children. At the end of the tale Werfel spins, the leader was left deserted, betrayed; his grand mission concluded by a fatal shot from a Turkish soldier. He died on the grave of his beloved son.

The sanitary conditions got worse. Not only were the latrines almost entirely unusable, but there was no more potable water. Yossi stood on the bridge and perhaps in jest—since he had no other weapon—gave the order on the megaphone: "From now on, sickness is forbidden!" In the belly of the ship, a pipe of running salt water saved the youngsters from the heat of the nearby engine room.

Again a British bomber appeared, and again they all fled for cover. Again the Englishman signaled, repeating his request for identification. By now it was obvious there was no point in playing games. Nevertheless Yossi answered that the ship's name was *St. Anna*, and it was sailing for Alexandretta to pick up a cargo of cotton and bring it to Port Said.

The moment the plane disappeared, they began to dismantle everything on deck: they threw the shower stalls into the sea, and anything flammable was taken below to the boiler room for kindling. It was necessary they give the impression that this was truly a merchant ship on its regular route, though that was a long shot. Suddenly two destroyers burst out of the darkness. Knowing he had nothing more to lose, Yossi summoned the refugees onto the deck. The British signaled in Morse not to incite the crowd against them. "You are breaking the law," they declared. And Yossi replied that their ship, *Jewish Resistance*, was sailing to Palestine, and its people would fight like lions against anyone who interfered.

Meanwhile they had already passed Tyre, with the British destroyers alongside. Someone came to the bridge and told Yossi that his friend had jumped into the sea, thinking he could swim ashore. Seventeen miles separated them and the shore. Yossi rushed to the wheels and turned the ship 180 degrees around. The British couldn't make any sense of it. He notified them by wireless that there was a man overboard. One of the destroyers tore off on a rescue mission at a speed of twenty-seven knots, its bow extending from the water like a racing boat. It shot like an arrow, leaving a lengthy wake behind. Sitting on the *Jewish Resistance*, which crawled along like a tortoise, Yossi watched the enemy zip through the sea and realized how naive they were to have thought they could storm their way to the shore. In half an hour the British announced from the destroyer, "We have the missing man, and he is hale and healthy."

Yossi had no intention of surrendering, and everything continued as if nothing had happened—the destroyer remained close, never letting up, nearly touching the sides of the ship, and on deck the wails of the sirens could be heard. Yossi read the statements he had in his hands over the megaphone about their right to a homeland. But the English from their side demanded unconditional surrender.

When the British issued an exceptional request to deliver a message directly to all the refugees, Yossi consented without any difficulty. The announcement was transmitted by loudspeakers full blast: "If you approach the shores of Palestine, we will attack. Do you need any medical assistance?" And as in some children's game, Yossi answered: "We are considering your announcement with all our passengers." The British replied: "Any attempt to reach territorial waters will amount to a breach of the law, resulting in arrest." And Yossi began an emotional sermon: "The people here have come from German concentration camps in Europe, and we have no intention of transferring them to British concentration camps. Do you think we set out on this journey as if it were a pleasure cruise on the *Queen Mary*? More than three thousand women, men, and children are aboard this small ship, in subhuman conditions. Can you possibly imagine the pain and suffering of these women? The agony of those who have given birth? Are we criminals? Why are you hunting us down like wild animals? Sirs, can you possibly think that anybody in his right mind would willingly choose to enter a concentration camp, even if it is British? We will fight for our right to live. We will defend ourselves in any way we can—with our bodies, with our bare hands, with bottles, with sticks, with pipes, with gasoline."

Yossi's choice of words was effective and prudent, unforgetting and unforgettable. His choice of words was designed to underscore that here it was a question of David versus Goliath. Like an orator, but also like someone who tells things as they are, he quoted the words of Churchill, which perfectly suited that moment: "We shall fight on the shore, we shall fight on the streets, we shall fight on the decks of ships."

The British ignored the content of his words and announced dryly: "This conflict will only make matters worse." And then somebody else began to speak: "This is the commander speaking. Great Britain has fought for the freedom of the entire world and rescued it from the jaws of Nazi occupation. It would not be correct for you to perturb public opinion. Britain has consistently shown herself to be your good friend." Yossi did not reply. The enormous and menacing destroyer was already up close, sailing only a few meters from the deck. The crowd shouted at the soldiers: "Palestine! Palestine!"

The destroyers toyed with the ship, approaching and backing off again and again. Their movement in the water raised the level of the waves and jostled the ship. The officers in white helmets were clearly visible and threateningly close. The shore already loomed on the horizon. *Anna* now sailed at full speed— four knots—as the destroyer constantly maneuvered around it. While Yossi tried to solve the logistical problem, he did not forget for a moment that most of the wooden materials on the ship had already been consumed in the furnace and there was nowhere to sit or sleep, that people were sick, that salt water had begun to penetrate the antiquated water system. But, by the same token, he did not forget that it was forbidden to let the British see or know their situation. He continued to oscillate between despair and hope that the Jewish army, the very army about which the children on the ship sang at the bidding of the leaders from the youth movements, would come from the increasingly close shores of Palestine and help them. He prayed: "May Hanita come. May Tel Amal come. May the Haganah come. May the Irgun come. May the Palmach come. May somebody come."

And from the other side, the leadership in Palestine conducted a seemingly petty debate: What name should they give the ship? Anxious pointed telegrams arrived with the instruction to alter the provocative name of the ship, *Jewish Resistance*, to *Knesset Israel*.

Amnon, Yossi Harel, refused. The name did not speak to the heart, and in the midst of his difficult predicament he tried to argue, persuade, clarify that precisely now, precisely for the enfeebled foolhardy refugees, this name was very significant. But he did not have a choice. He was told point-blank that the decision was not negotiable. Someone climbed onto the prow and inscribed the new name, *Knesset Israel*. In the distance appeared the mountains of Galilee and Carmel. Yossi explained to all those aboard ship at length, and with love, what they were looking at, though he already knew that shortly they would all be boarded on deportation ships. They stood on the deck, and Yossi reported to the council that a *habeas corpus* had already been submitted to the high court on their behalf and that the attorney for the Jewish agency, Dr. Bernard Yosef, the future Minister Dov Yosef, had received the roster of passengers and was getting ready to sue the government for unauthorized denial of liberty.

Now they were already without food, without water, and without fuel. So with no choice, like Samson among the Philistines, Yossi ordered that they enter the port. In the messages that he transmitted from the ship, he turned directly to the headquarters of the Haganah and the Palmach: "We are making every preparation for disembarkation. You promised you would be on the shore, you must organize stiff opposition. We intend to force the community to fight for the refugees and to become actively engaged on behalf of the survivors."

In the subsequent clash there would be one fatality, a boy of sixteen, and scores of wounded, including many British, but the fighting units of the Jewish community, the community Yossi now turned to with his desperate cry for help, was not there. The harbor docks were deserted. No Palmach, no Haganah, no multitudes that were supposed to greet the faces of their returning brethren, and all the while Yossi, his heart broken and torn apart, was ordering the human fragments with him to fight back.

At the entrance to the bay, the destroyers came within centimeters of the ship, and strong sailors armed with clubs leaped onto the deck and took up strategic positions. The commander of the marine unit entered the communications cabin. Haifa was spread out before them. On its rooftops appeared hordes of people. *Knesset Israel*, already without a drop of fuel, food, or water, groaned its last, was tied to the pier, and all that remained was to refuse to lower the gangplank. The destroyers anchored up against it. The wharf was swarming with marines, British police, and *ghaffirs*, Arab supernumerary constables.

With the command "Attack!" reverberating in English from the loudspeaker, the British began to climb up ladders they attached to the ship. Violently repulsed by the refugees, they fell into the water. Three squads of marines stormed one after another—and failed. The refugees were hardened, angry, and desperate. The terrors of their twenty-three-day odyssey along their own *Via Dolorossa* now erupted like lava. They madly hurled the ladders at the British ships. On the left, *Empire Highwood* had already anchored, the ship that served to deport Jewish refugees to Cyprus. Now another ship arrived, crammed with British sailors. All the while Yossi wondered where the representatives of the Jewish agency could possibly be.

The order to disembark was again heard from the loudspeaker on the wharf. And another British attempt to take control failed. There was a brief lull. Yossi pondered. The British pondered. And then the signal for the second stage was given: a mighty salvo of tear gas was launched onto the ship. There were hundreds of explosives, and the stifling atmosphere was unbearable. Nearly 4,500 people crowded the deck—these were the fighters—and in the hold of the ship in storerooms were all the rest, 2,500 men, women, infants one day old, the sick, and the elderly. Some of the canisters that fell on the deck rolled down to the storerooms. A terrible panic seized everyone. Like swarming bees, choking, vomiting, they tried to climb out—to breathe—trampling anyone in their path. And the exploding canisters kept landing. Eyes teared, flesh scorched, hair caught on fire, and the canisters kept coming.

Squad after squad, in gas masks and helmets, the British tried to place ladders to climb on to the deck, but the fighters—their lungs seared—still fought like lions, throwing at them whatever they could lay their hands on, tin cans, iron bars, nails, anything they could grab from the ship. Those who could not withstand the smoke and fire jumped into the sea, screaming for their lives, from a height of twelve meters, where they were picked up by patrol boats lurking in the area to trap their prey.

The clatter of machine guns continued nonstop. More salvos of tear gas. The ship filled with smoke. A canister rolled into the babies' room. The mothers shrieked. Yossi managed to grab the canister and toss it back into the sea, where it exploded.

The ship was completely enveloped in smoke and fumes. Sardine cans were an insufficient response to the tear gas and machine guns. After people were forcibly removed, they lay on the docks, scorched and breathing with difficulty. The remainder in the hold of the ship climbed to the deck with their last bit of strength and collapsed unconscious. They were beaten and dragged in anger to the DDT installations for disinfection and from there to the deportation ships.

Two hundred meters separated them from Palestine. A few refugees extricated themselves for a moment from the clutches of the British soldiers and kissed the filthy docks on which they were briefly allowed to tread before being kicked to the deportation boats.

Then a sad girl came onto the deck, with a number seared into her chest, an old guitar in her hand, and her name, *Feldhure A. 13652*—as if none of this had anything to do with her, as though she, her name, and her guitar were all that existed—and she sang on the deck: "Sleep, valley of a glorious land . . . " The English approached with an even taller ship and opened fire. She was not hit. And although by that point there was already a second fatality, and another cry for help had been sounded accordingly, Haifa had not yet sent an army. The smoke billowed upward, but *Feldhure A. 13652* would not come down; they beat her, but she would not budge. She sat and sang.

The British were strong and young. Facing them were 3,845 choking and scorched refugees. The British took up positions on the trounced ship and continued to brutally remove the refugees to the deportation ships. The elderly first, then women and mothers holding on tightly to their children. And on the other side, on the deportation deck, stood British officers with hatred and contempt blazoned on their faces, handing out biscuits and water to the refugees.

As they departed toward evening on the deportation ship, Yossi lifted his eyes. Opposite him he could already see the lights of Carmel turning on, one after another. A mountain strewn with stars. Through the wire grid spreading over them, the mountain grew smaller and smaller, and the lights seemed like weeping diamonds. Yossi wore a leather coat, a Russian hat, and boots. The British searched for the ship commander. They never imagined this young refugee could be he. He was stuck inside the holding pen's inhuman congestion under an iron net, on one of the three ships, among 1,400 refugees. There was a sour odor of used clothing, old dry suffering, sweat, a variety of human naphthalene, dull and dismal. A profound despair hung over them, but at its edge there was a fragile shamed spark of hope, and from all this anguish, despondency, and pain rose once again the voice of a sad girl with a number seared in her chest, an old guitar in her hand—as if all this did not concern her. "Oh, my Kinneret," came from her throat. Afterward, silence. One thousand four hundred people, human fragments, in a pen floating slowly, quietly—opposite sparkling, fading lights—and moving farther and farther from the land it never reached.

And from the storerooms at the bottom of the pen to the decks above rose an echoing song, a whisper at first, then a roar, 1,400 people singing and weeping.

* * *

It was a disappointment, they said. The *land,* they said, not the *land of Israel. "Min geyt tsum erets,"* they said. "We're going to the land." On the floating pen, the refugees declared a hunger strike. The British did not permit them to move around, except to go to the latrines, and even then only with an escort. They stood behind the nets of their sailing prisons and kept up their hunger strike. Contempt and disgust poured from the eyes of the British, but the strike worked. The British conceded to the utterly human demand of the refugees, permitting them to move around. The hunger strike halted, and negotiations over the granting of humane conditions began.

Meanwhile Yitzhak Artzi and Yossi organized a protest against disembarkation on the shores of Cyprus, where they could already see from afar a procession of children in tattered clothing, led by a child carrying a torn flag, singing on their way to a new concentration camp. But the protest failed to achieve the goal, and Yossi was the last to disembark. They loaded everybody on trucks straight into an area of tent camps and barracks situated about ten kilometers from the port. The camp was also surrounded by spiky barbed-wire fences. Already incarcerated in it were twelve thousand refugees brought from previous ships. The British thought nobody could escape from there.

As soon as he arrived, Yossi met members of the Palmach coming in the guise of doctors or nurses from Palestine or as emissaries from the Joint Distribution Committee—an organization authorized officially by the British to deal with refugees. In one of the tents there was a secret underground wireless set that had been smuggled out of Palestine and reassembled on the spot. Contact with Palestine was continuously maintained.

The camp was well run, the food reasonable, and schools established to teach Hebrew. Muted passion blossomed there; all the people wanted to do was give birth, continue the race in spite of those who had tried to eradicate it from the face of the earth, to start fresh.

After a month 750 refugees left Cyprus for Palestine, only half the number of certificates that should have been authorized by the British. Yossi was lucky. Two days after he arrived, they issued the certificates. Yossi Harel returned to Palestine a fully legal immigrant, on his way to the next venture.

Chapter Eleven

T he voyage of the *Knesset Israel* lacked the dramatic political flavor that would turn the *Exodus* into a symbol and a legend, but it established the fact that no British fleet could prevail against the will to come home.

From Haifa, Yossi traveled by bus to Tel Aviv. As soon as he arrived he went to Café Kasit, and from there he telephoned Yitzhak Sadeh at his penthouse on Rothschild Boulevard, and Sadeh invited him over at once. Sadeh served wine and cheese, and Yossi related what had occurred at the departure and at the port. Trying to keep his voice devoid of the anguished fury he felt, he let him know how he felt about a child dying aboard ship while the Jews in Palestine sat as if nothing had happened. "I'm a Haganah agent, but I must speak here in the name of the refugees, for I consider myself one of them. Why did you not bring the youth of Ein-Harod to fight? If they had done that, at least, perhaps I would have responded to the Palmach's request and allowed the children on the ship to keep on fighting."

He described the events of the voyage from beginning to end. He went day by day, growing more and more stunned by what he had gone through. Sadeh listened quietly. Deflated, he asked Yossi to be at Café Kasit on Friday night.

Friday arrived, and Yossi went to Kasit. Hezkel, the proprietor, closed the café. Sadeh had also invited Hannah Rovina, Shlonsky, Alterman, Bat Miriam, Maskin, Tsilah Bender, and a few other members of Palestine's intellectual establishment. Once they drank and ate, Sadeh bade them all sit down and said, "I want you to hear from the mouth of the *Knesset Israel* commander the story of its voyage." Yossi began slowly, letting the story tell itself; he was no longer at the café, but on the deck, and the eyes of almost four thousand people were gazing at him, speaking with his voice. The betrayal they had suffered at the hands of Jewish leaders of Palestine expressed itself through his voice, as did the bravery of the survivors who had bitten soldiers, had been beaten half to death, and now sat in camps on Cyprus. With the deep rage of a Jerusalemite, Yossi spoke about the tear gas, the floating orphanage, the clash, and how it ended with all of them defeated. He spoke of how some jumped from a height of ten meters into the sea without even knowing how to swim; how British police boats collected them; how they were all lowered one after the other, were made to pass through a cycle of disinfection with DDT, and were immediately loaded onto deportation ships.

He spoke about the congestion. About sleeves that got rolled up aboard ship, about the ballet of blue numbers sparkling in the murky light, about a woman who'd told him how her baby had been shot to death by Nazis and tossed into the gutter. And he said that despite everything, each of those people was ready to die on the ship's deck as long as someone would reach some destination. He recalled a girl who had hidden herself the moment she saw that her body cast a shadow, mumbling Catholic prayers— spectral, weighing just thirty-three kilos. Her waxen legs that had frozen in the snow could now barely move. She had tried to smile and said, "Even my smile was dead till now."

The silence in the room was total. The pulse in their veins could be heard. Nobody moved, as though any movement would disrupt something. Yossi expressed profound bitterness over the way the fight at the harbor was left to the survivors of the Holocaust, and nobody from the Haganah, from the Haifa workers, or from the Palmach had come down to the port to join them in their clash with the British.

"I was already used to firing a machine gun in Hanita. I fought. Did I ever expect elderly survivors of Auschwitz to fight for me? In this land, the survivors should be the last and not the first to carry on the struggle against the British."

He paused for a moment, then went on to say: "When I returned to Haifa, members of the Palmach and Aliyah Beth were waiting for me, including Yigal Alon. They obviously knew about my coming from Cyprus. We sat in one of the restaurants, and I gave them a firsthand report on what we went through during twenty-three days at sea. They heard about all this for the first time. I told them about the engagement with the British at the port, about the tear gas that penetrated through the ship's stern and endangered the lives of mothers and their babies. I didn't conceal from them my rage over their absence."

And he went on: "If they had just organized a demonstration to encourage the refugees . . . But they did nothing, zero. These refugees, these remnants of the Jewish people, actually reached Haifa—and Haifa went about its business as usual, as though nothing were wrong. And at the harbor the refugees fought against the British alone."

The listeners were hearing of this odyssey for the first time.

The poet Nathan Alterman rose in a fury and began to mutter to himself. Yossi continued and told how they had buried the infant in a crate of canned goods, covered it in tarpaulin, and tied it with the chains of the anchor. He spoke for four hours without a stop. "Somebody has to tell me why the refugees should fight if nobody on shore fights. They are survivors, they come from hell. Why should they be the ones to sacrifice themselves? Why all over again? The order not to put up a fight should have been given, because any opposition means bloodshed—and it's not right for refugees to fight while here the people sit at coffeehouses. When Yigal Alon gave me his answer, that the blood of refugees was the blood of fighters who sacrificed themselves in a war to free their people, I shook at the sound of his words."

He felt empty and depleted upon finishing his story. Hezkel handed him a glass. They all rose. Nobody opened his mouth, and without consulting each other they left in several taxis for the Dolphin Bar. Menashe Baharev played his accordion. Hannah Rovina sat in a corner, shut her eyes, and began singing in Russian, and as she sang she wept, she sang and she wept. Her voice in Russian could shatter glass.

Shlonsky asked Yossi, "What now?" And Yossi said he was leaving at once to bring another ship. Shlonsky quoted the line "My creatures are drowning at sea and you sing songs?"—a line that, according to Jewish legend, God said to the angels when they extolled Him at the sight of the Egyptians drowning in the Red Sea. Yossi listened. Contentious God had more compassion for the Egyptians than his friends had for those who waited at the seaports of the Mediterranean in order to reach a place they could call their home, a place where they could perhaps speak with people from their towns, from their childhood, and join the world of the living through memories in new places they knew nothing about. Alterman listened and kept quiet. The following Friday he published, in the *Seventh Column*, his poem "The Division of Duties."

> Then the girl began to run! Up in the air!
> To the ship that was waiting to deport her
> But she suddenly recalled what I, the yishuv,
> Commanded: Stop, don't move, not yet.
>
> But just one thing she may not have known
> And may come to me in complaint.
> What was the task that she was assigned?
> And what was mine that day?
>
> And perhaps she would add
> A word here or there
> In the name of her friends and the young
> How it was wrong to ask them to do
> What the yishuv did not ask of itself.

Witness the way of survivors
Witness the wet eyes of their young
When tasks were assigned
Not according to strength.

After the stormy encounter, Yossi went home. He changed his clothes—it was already quite late—and slept on a bench on Ben-Zion Avenue near his room, since he was afraid he would not wake up in time. Before sunrise, at five o'clock, they would pick him up for his next mission, to bring the *Exodus*.

Chapter Twelve

In June of 1947, early in the morning, following the "night of poetry" organized by Yitzhak Sadeh, Yossi left Haifa along with two friends. The three were brought by a fishing boat to the small Greek cargo ship that was waiting for them. They hid in the room that housed the rusty anchors. After the ship set out to sea, they came on deck all blackened with soot and dirt. Upon reaching Italy's territorial waters, they followed the same procedure. They were lowered into a little boat awaiting them at the entrance to Naples. Then they took a train to Milan.

They reached the illegal immigration base headed then by Yehudah Arazi, a virtuoso and daredevil of Aliyah Beth and one of its first heroes who in 1946, under the name of Dr. Do Paz, had joined the refugees besieged on the *Dov Hos* and led their struggle aboard ship. He had distributed "official" Palestine immigration documents bearing the words "To you and to your descendants I shall give the land" and "With enormous compassion I shall gather them," plus the text of the Balfour Declaration, and alerted journalists he knew to publicize the affair.

Arazi was situated in an office in the Jewish community. Numerous Aliyah Beth outposts were scattered throughout Italy at that time, but command headquarters was in Rome because of the necessary and unavoidable contacts with local authorities. Ada Sereni, an elegant, beautiful, and impressive woman whom Yossi knew and admired, handled the relations with local authorities very effectively. An Italian aristocrat and member of Kibbutz Givat Brenner, Sereni tied her fate with Palestine. She worked in Aliyah Beth as an emissary of the kibbutz. The daughter of a man who had at one time served as personal physician to the king of Italy, she had connections and inroads to the nobility and local high society. The Communists, who considered her a valiant underground fighter, also initiated contacts and helped out when they could.

On the first evening in Milan, Yossi told Arazi and Ada Sereni the story of *Knesset Israel* and what had occurred in Haifa Bay. Shaken, Arazi defined the journey as "an irresponsible act." To board four thousand people on such a pathetic ship . . . what if all four thousand of them had drowned?

Yossi did not agree. Their argument was over fundamental principles. Arazi was a believer in small ships. Yossi, like Avigur, wanted to save as many as possible in the shortest amount of time as possible.

In the end, their argument proved irrelevant. The decisive factor was the increasing pressure of the Jews who wanted to reach Palestine at nearly any cost.

Yossi was assigned to meet the huge ship that was to serve as the vessel for the next mission. But as the ship's departure from the United States had been delayed, he went to northern Italy, not far from Milan, to visit a small village that served as a base for various activities of the Palestine Jews. Formerly an ammunition depot of the Jewish Brigade, the place had been transformed into a refugee camp. It still stored a large cache of arms, booty from organized raids on British army camps, concealed in Italian compressors and steamrollers ordered by Solel-Boneh, a Jewish construction company in Palestine.

While engaged in the loading process, he was informed that Shaul Avigur wanted to see him. They met in a small coffeehouse in Milan. Shaul was a short man who looked like a priest disguised as a failed businessman. His appearance was somewhat deceiving. This powerful man, familiar with leadership by virtue of his worldview and the role several members of his family played in the community, was a bundle of painful, explosive memories. Avigur, in the vanguard of the camp, a courageous and daring visionary, lived and conducted himself on a daily basis under the cloud of the *Patria*. Ever since that disastrous operation, Avigur analyzed, checked, and rechecked each and every activity. As a man of the field—Ben-Gurion's factotum—he arrived in Milan to meet Yossi.

From Avigur's expression, Yossi sensed that something important was about to transpire. Avigur informed him that an American ship called the *President Warfield*—large, but quite fast—had finally arrived in Porto Venere and that Yossi had been appointed its commander.

The Jewish American crew of volunteers to Mossad le-Aliyah Beth, including a young captain named Ike Aharonowitz, had fitted the antiquated pleasure boat in Baltimore, then transported it down the Potomac to Norfolk, Virginia, where they made some renovations, spread the rumor that their destination was Hong Kong, and secretly set sail. But the ship broke down, forcing them to bring it back for repairs. After these additional repairs, the antiquated riverboat was discreetly cut loose once again and this time made it across the ocean.

Two hours after their meeting, Yossi, Avigur, and Signora Sereni drove to Porto Venere, where they beheld a ship that loomed gigantic. The passenger decks were piled one on top of the other, and its menacing smokestack stretched upward. The ship was larger and seemed far more stable than all the ones they had known so far. Shaul asked the crew, which counted three Palestine Jews among the majority of Jewish American volunteers, including Ike Aharonowitz, to meet with Yossi.

The preparations for the voyage took much longer than planned. The political clock was ticking, and there was additional pressure of adverse weather conditions and the deteriorating circumstances of the camp residents who were anxious to begin the journey.

The Italians were feared to be playing a double game. In order not to risk their compromising the operation, Avigur concluded that rather than set sail from Italy, they should exploit the political conjunction of events in France and transport the refugees from there. Léon Blum, the Socialist Jew, himself a former prisoner of Buchenwald, was the French prime minister at the time. Given that grace period, it was possible to set sail from France, even though the French for the most part—save for the Communist underground and Socialists from the days of the Resistance—preferred collaboration with the British over helping survivors.

The chief mechanic, a Pole, notified Yossi that the amount of fuel was insufficient for the voyage to Port de Bouc in southern France. The British shadowed all their activities, spied through binoculars from the roofs of tall buildings, engaged collaborators from the local residents, and went on full alert before the operation even began. They informed the Shell Company, which was partly owned by British intelligence, not to supply the ship with oil. To enable them to set sail from the port, Ada Sereni came up with a temporary solution that was brilliant, bold, and simple: The side of the hill facing the anchored ship was studded with olive trees, so Sereni arranged for several dozen tankers to be placed at nightfall under the trees. The tankers in the olive orchard did not arouse suspicion. A long pipe stretched across the road to the ship, and the olive oil passed from the orchard to the boat. Now it could at least reach the French port.

Ladders, large rafts, and oil designated for spraying were placed all around the boat, measures of counterattack against soldiers attempting to board from decks of ships, so as to withstand the British destroyers if and when the boat got close to the shores of Palestine.

Compared with the *Knesset Israel*, the *President Warfield* was well armed and capable of reaching a speed of eighteen knots. It had kitchens, large halls, and ventilation. Yossi decided to test an evasive maneuver on the voyage to the French coast. Under the cover of fog, they silenced the motors and halted the ship all at once. After the heavy Italian destroyer that had been shadowing them on behalf of the British glided by, they started up again, turned the boat ninety degrees to the right toward the coast, and sailed full speed ahead.

They succeeded in shaking off the destroyer.

Chapter Thirteen

On July 11, 1947, the *President Warfield* arrived at Port de Bouc in southwestern France. After entering the port, the crew met Shmariah Zamereth, who had been engaged in illegal immigration work for many years and was rich in experience. Shmariah showed up in a raft loaded with barrels of oil amounting to enough fuel to cross the Mediterranean. Meanwhile Yossi learned he could expect 4,500 rather than 4,000 refugees. He was not yet told from which port they would depart.

Although the ship seemed large, it was no more than 330 feet long. The operation itself required a complicated logistics involving the renting of trains and trucks and the setting up of transit camps wherein they would gather the refugees, then divide them into separate groups. It was necessary to train instructors, commanders, and orderlies. They found themselves in an open area, under the watchful eyes of an enemy that daily lay in wait for them. They had to devise a detailed strategy so as to outwit the powerful, untrammeled foe and prepare the refugees for the voyage. But they also had to wait until the ship was ready.

In Port de Bouc Yossi received the message to sail to the nearby port of Sète, from where they would depart. The French government had authorized passage for two groups of refugees from Germany through France. Each group numbered about 1,250 persons. The organizers collected the transit permits at two border stations selected in advance and used the same permits twice on two different nights, thus doubling the total number of refugees that crossed the border.

When the refugees reached France, they boarded trains and were transported to the preparation camps, located for the time being in southern France. Having already been assembled in camps in Italy as well as in some small villages in southern France, the refugees were now housed in twelve camps around Marseilles.

In these camps waited 1,282 women, 1,561 men, 1,017 adolescents, and 655 children. Among the Palestine Jews working in the camps, established thanks to the winking eyes of the French, were Saul Biber and Micah Perry, who trained the youngsters to supervise the camps on their own and even prepare the adults for embarkation. Yossi toured the camps. He wanted to feel the people out, to be certain they were ready for the project and had received all that was available to them. Over and over he saw the sorrow, the hunger, and the pain that gaped like an open wound in the surviving body of the Jewish people.

In one of these camps near Marseilles hundreds of children, most of them orphans, were assembled. At this juncture the saga of the *Exodus* is strewn with the eyes of these orphans about to board the ship. Their eyes held the dream, the wisdom, the fabric, the text from which this saga is made; eyes, all of them full of suffering, and some dull of hope, slender as it may have been. These were the eyes of children who were furious at the God of their forefathers, the God who, they felt and said, had abandoned them; the eyes of those now awaiting Yossi, the Jewish officer from Palestine, with hope, pride, and renewed strength.

These eyes, brown, blue, deep, glazed, these piercing eyes are the real story of the *Exodus*, even before the ship became a symbol. More than eight thousand eyes that had seen the incredible would later embark on the ship, and Yossi, upon meeting the children, was already unsure of himself. Among them he felt small, but for their sake he tried to appear like a hero because they wanted him to be one, the mythical soldier of an imaginary state. This encounter with what he called thereafter and for the rest of his life the "orphanages" was fateful. The *Exodus* was the momentary opening of eyes to catch sight of a future that was visible and not simply memorialize a past that was indescribable.

It seemed strange to Yossi not to find any adults there—no fathers, no mothers, just children, all by themselves. Some had survived because they managed to pass themselves off as non-Jews. The little ones, who didn't speak a good enough Polish in their monastery hideouts, were gathered by the older children, who protected them by a secret code. Even the nuns, who hid them, had difficulty figuring out what was going on and how it worked. Yossi stood stunned before this rare fraternity of the condemned. They had saved each other in the forests, among the partisans, in the monasteries. All of them—nuns and children alike—had been hungry. There had been no wood for heating. In the hideaways, under such difficult conditions, the non-Jewish children were likely to be tempted to scapegoat the Jewish children for a loaf of bread. The German soldiers had lain in wait by the monasteries because they suspected Jewish children were hidden inside. It became clear to Yossi that in these monastery hideouts the older children took turns during the night staying awake in order to prevent a child from prattling in Yiddish while asleep.

The mutual devotion of the children among whom Yossi now found himself was a classified, indecipherable document. What Yossi wanted was to crack this secret code and figure out how to comfort these children. But what stood out even more clearly was the enormity of the responsibility placed upon him. Trust was the last thing they felt toward anybody, yet that was exactly what they chose to offer him. For them, survival was a subject fraught with obstacles. In their short lives they had learned only one thing, whom to trust and whom not to trust. Sometimes it was a matter of life or death. Sometimes the wrong choice was made, and nobody was left to reveal the consequences.

In contrast, they also met other Jews from Palestine educated to loathe the history of the Jews. They met more than a few Palestine Jews who considered them human worms and believed that anyone who survived had committed a moral crime. For other Jews from Palestine, they were simply merchandise to be shipped to Palestine. Even when the children banded together, they were more isolated than any other children Yossi had ever met. These children stuck to each other. Some had seen their parents die before their own eyes or watched them disappear. The nuns noted the password that the Jewish children whispered to a new child, but they couldn't understand how they identified or recognized each other and what the password was. Perhaps, thought Yossi, it was "*Shema Yisroel.*" But actually these youngsters, children at the time, came mainly from secular homes of assimilated Jewish intelligentsia in Poland. There were rabbis who did not permit their children to be collected and saved at the hands of nuns, instead letting them die what they called a "sanctification of the name." So these children were the only ones left. The others had perished.

They told him how the older ones had warned them not to cross themselves too often, so as not to arouse suspicion. They related how one girl had called out, "Daddy, where are you? Daddy, take me from here, this death will kill me." She'd identified the white robes of the nuns with death. And now they fixed their eyes on Yossi, as though they wanted to see when he would break, or would hit them, or become like one of them.

Yossi thought he could detect a certain mysterious smile on their faces, a challenge that lay beyond the horror they described. Neither to wallow in suffering nor to brag about it, but simply to catalog it, a sort of reenactment of the need to be loved. To say what could not be said. Afterward most of them would keep quiet for twenty years; their children would never hear these stories.

The poet Haim Gouri called his first documentary film *The 81st Blow*. The title derives from the testimony of Michael Goldmann-Gilead at the Eichmann trial: when Goldmann related that he had been whipped with eighty lashes, he was met with disbelief; people could not believe that anyone could survive after eighty lashes. So he repeated his story again. It was this shattering disbelief that he called "the eighty-first blow." Perhaps by the same principle, the children repeatedly unveiled their portraits of hell on the walls of a transitory, pathetic paradise, facing precisely someone they thought would understand them. They considered, it seemed, provocation a form of victory. They wanted Yossi to be worthy of the trust they placed in him and to love them. What could the Jewish officer from Palestine know about hiding a piece of bread? What could he know about lice? What could he know about saying prayers in a church with Germans swarming all around it—genuinely praying to a God that was not yours?

Yossi's encounter with the "orphanages" in the camp, before embarkation onto the *Exodus*, revived his own painful childhood, for every child wants a mother's kiss and a father's guidance. Many of these children had met good-hearted nuns who risked themselves to rescue them, partisans, farmers with a conscience. But they had also met all the others. Some would never forgive their parents because, in their child's imagination, they felt abandoned by their parents who perished in the camps. They always felt guilty, as if they were unlovable or unworthy, and for that reason were neglected by those who should have loved them.

Yossi found it easy to identify with them. He had no need to play the mythical Jewish sabra from Palestine, silent and strong. They learned the rules of the game soon enough but remained cautious. For some of them, the first religion they encountered in their lives was Christianity. One of them was angry at the God of his grandfather for abandoning them, so he loved Jesus, who saved him. Another girl explained how she embraced any anti-Semitic Christian prayer, embraced it even though she was surprised how angry she was at herself.

There was a girl there who said she had been looking for her relatives since she was eleven years old. She never found them, but she did find a woman who had once worked for her father. The woman dyed the girl's hair blond and sent her to an orphanage. She fled from there and lived in damp cellars and got sick. "I came to a hospital," she said, "as a Christian girl. One of the nuns pitied me. Did she know? I'll never know."

She was taken to a monastery. There were other Jews there who immediately recognized that she was Jewish. At the end of the war a tall, elegant woman came by to take her to Lodz. She said that before the war the girl's name was Rivkah. The girl didn't believe her. The woman said, "You are Rivkah. You are Rivkah." The nuns argued on behalf of the girl and said she had to go sing in a choir rehearsal, but the woman persisted; she gave the nuns money and took her away. Rivkah wept and swore to the nuns that she would return to the monastery. She did not return; she was taken to the camp to board the *Exodus*.

Yossi haggled with all sorts of petty merchants and bought sweets for the youngsters. In exchange they showed him the possessions they dragged along with them—prayer beads, crosses. Each one of them seemed to have kept some talisman, and they came to Palestine with these possessions. "All we knew," they said, "was that we were different, rejected by our parents and despised by God."

They asked Yossi, "What's freedom? What is it for? What does it look like? Will we get separated from each other again?" Always together, they were their own family. They remembered how, after the war ended, people would come to take them. The children were suspicious of such strangers and did not want to accompany them. There were so many Jews who had lost children in the camps, and they would come to the monasteries for the purpose of claiming children as their own.

Most of them could hardly remember what a real home looked like from the inside or how a bed looked in a bedroom. Nor could they remember what warmth and love were, what a city in which you lived looked like, as opposed to one in which you merely loitered in its vicinity. They knew the world only as lodgers for the night or as passengers on a boat with a glass bottom in a sea of sewage. In their two-year-long flight throughout Europe they did whatever they could: they bought and sold gold teeth of the dead, rings, eggs, condoms. They held on to each other tightly.

Yossi's quiet strength and tenderness seemed to constitute the answer to the muffled longing for revenge that nested in their hearts, the answer to their loss of all values. Surviving had meant breaking the law. They wanted to know if there was any reason to stop fighting, if there was anything in the world for which it was not just worth surviving, but worth living; in Yossi they found a listening ear. They told him it was impossible to explain what they had experienced to someone who wasn't there—nobody would understand or want to understand. Nobody would believe it. He said that he perhaps would not understand, but he wanted to try.

Miriam Cohen, a small, delicate, Aryan-looking girl, told about her flight from the ghetto. She sat facing Yossi, her blazing expression making him feel as though she saw right through him. Her body crouched in a quasi reflex of fear. Even so, the corners of her mouth rose in an expression of domesticated, partially appeased, anger. She spoke slowly. Outside it was already evening, and the searchlights were on.

She related that after her escape from the ghetto she rode aimlessly on the trolley cars. At night she hid in stairwells and survived by selling the bread she stole to the Polish inmates of a nearby camp, letting on that she was bringing bread for her father, though in actuality she had seen him being taken out to be shot.

As she traveled the trolleys, she signaled to Jewish youngsters that they should flee. One of them fell in love with her. He escaped the commando unit whose ranks he had joined and searched for her. He was caught but didn't betray her. Occasionally her identity was discovered, and she had to flee. She disguised herself as a German, said her home was destroyed and her parents killed by Russians on the eastern front. Luckily she had spoken German back in Galicia. Near Munich she met an older man whom she came to trust, and he raped her. She became infected with a disease and went to a doctor, who suspected she was Jewish but took pity on her and let her continue to flee.

At the end of the war she reached a transit camp and entered the "Halutz" orphanage. After traveling by foot for a year, she reached Italy. From there she traveled intermittently by truck until she reached France. And now, at the age of seventeen, Miriam Cohen was waiting to board the *President Warfield*.

In the general formation, they slung their packs over their shoulders, trying to appear "ready" for the soldier from Palestine. He saw how people carried loaves of bread around with them everywhere; even on the ship, despite their hunger, they held on to their bread and wouldn't eat it. He saw how they always kept something with them, something from home, not necessarily their actual home, an imagined home—a cross, prayer beads, a candlestick, a ring, a small candelabrum, a faded photograph. Yossi felt from then on that the task he was taking upon himself was sacred.

And while they still waited, in one of the barracks in the camp, Yossi met Yatsek, a boy who had removed shoes from the dead, and with the money earned he would purchase not just bread but newspapers to cover the corpses. He related that in the deportation of the Jews of Plassov in May of 1944, he saw how Jews were transported to the railway cars, where a pajama-clad orchestra was playing spirited tangos, and after they too were sent to the concentration camp, gramophones looted from Jewish homes were brought in to play waltzes and marching songs for them.

One of the children was a rabbi's son, named Moshe. He was saved and raised in a monastery. When they found him, he went temporarily insane from what he was told. And another boy related how, at age nine, he was thrown by his parents from a moving train full of Jews, thrown packed in a suitcase drilled with holes so he could breathe. Christian farmers found him and took care of him, and now he reached the transit camp carrying a small cross to bring to Jerusalem on behalf of his adoptive parents. Another described how he crawled from a mound of corpses after liberation and screamed, "Anybody alive? Anybody alive? Let somebody else be alive!?" And walking skeletons came out of the pile of corpses to devour the food brought by the liberators.

Y. Polak came from a rich and assimilated family in Warsaw. During the war he managed to conceal the fact that he was Jewish even while he was placed in a labor camp for Poles. After liberation he returned to Poland. He didn't find a single person from his family. The Poles who had confiscated his parents' home were cruel to him, because, they hissed, he "killed Christ." He fled to France, and now all he wanted to know and hear about was the Hebrew University in Jerusalem.

Chapter Fourteen

Once the construction of the four levels of bunks on each of the four decks of the *President Warfield* was completed, some of the refugees were brought in to help with the preparations. The force that had radiated from the Jews on the *Knesset Israel* while Yossi accompanied them throughout its capture, singing Yiddish songs with them, prepared him for this voyage. On that ship he felt humble like them, never sitting high on his pedestal as a sixth-generation Palestine Jew; he was merely being what they called in Yiddish a *gakhlits,* a new immigrant recruit, the scum of the earth. Quite simply, he'd been ready to do anything for them. "When I saw them I knew that nothing could stop us. I returned to the ship and saw only one thing before my eyes, the look on the faces of the children."

Yossi recalled that during the time he was Chaim Weizmann's chief bodyguard and confidant, he'd heard Weizmann tell of an incident that had occurred in the late thirties. The secretary of the British Mandate government, Sir John Shaw, who was not known as a lover of Zion, drove to Tiberias to unveil the tombstone of a British general. It was a scorching-hot day, dazzling, crystal clear, and oppressive. The Bedouins and Arabs found shelter in the shade of the houses and tents. Not a single vehicle could be seen on the steaming asphalt roads. Shaw felt as if he were about to faint. Near Kibbutz Afikim, he suddenly heard voices singing. The song was sung with fervor, with joy. He stopped the car to observe the marvel. In the banana plantation alongside the road, he saw scores of young women, new immigrants from Germany, very suntanned, but their white skin was nearly visible through their tan. They worked energetically, picking bananas in the blazing heat, singing enthusiastically in a language they could hardly speak. To himself he then said, not in regret but with open eyes, "The Jews, it seems, will win."

At this stage of the preparations for the embarking of the refugees, the French demanded visas. After much effort the Colombian consul agreed to supply visas for a considerable sum of money. But when he heard the number of people involved, he told them they might as well take the signets and stamp them themselves. To that end, they assembled those who had survived the German camps by forging dollars and sterling, the refugees whom the Germans had used as cogs in the economic war they waged against the Allies. In order to prepare the visas, they urgently needed photos of each of the refugees, so they enlisted scores of street photographers in Marseilles. They took them to the transit camp, and there they photographed those going on the voyage as well as people who just happened to be on the street. Then they printed thousands of documents. Thus, as was the case on the *Knesset Israel*, a man of fifty received a document bearing the photo of a child, and vice versa. But in the flood of people streaming by, who would notice which papers anybody held?

The French authorities, at the lower echelons, again began to get worried and toyed with the idea that perhaps the Jews with their Colombian visas could be sent to Colombia. The Colombians got scared and said that granting visas was one thing, but how the visas would be used was another. In about a week, through the intervention of the local Communists, a special and secret permit to set sail was issued. And the ship passed from port to port, trying to escape from one place to another, even including the option of turning to Barcelona if complications should arise.

Now the crew had to deal with a knotty logistical problem: how to transport 4,515 people from the transit camps near Marseilles to the port of Sète.

The logical solution was to rent enough trucks to carry everyone, but it just so happened that their departure coincided with a wave of strikes that had descended on France, and the truck drivers were part of that wave. The Communists leaned toward agreeing to the request of the Palestine Jews to break the strike, and the simultaneous contribution of a total of one million francs to the strike fund helped both sides. Thus was established the "British army" of truck drivers—150 members of the sham British unit, the TTG, for transporting the refugees and the rest for any emergency. It took precise planning and intricate logistical deployment. The transportation itself lasted many hours. These trucks that were "borrowed" from the British army had already plowed the roads of Europe innumerable times. They had a fair share of breakdowns, and now and again problems cropped up with police looking for a bribe. The long convoy was occasionally forced to split up on alternate routes in order not to call attention to itself. The trucks were covered in tarpaulin to conceal their cargo, and because of the stifling congestion inside the truck, people could barely breathe. To compound the challenge, the operation had to be accomplished under the cover of darkness. Yossi thought of Sadeh and Wingate and how even here it was necessary to exploit the night to win the day.

For the moment it seemed as if the Jewish nation were streaming toward the Mediterranean Sea. En route to the ship, Yossi saw trains with blue-and-white flags—apparently hand painted—waving in childish excitement and pride from the windows. The passengers knew full well how difficult the path was that awaited them, but after years of being wizards of survival, people who conned their way across frozen rivers, swamps, steep paths, hostile populations, hunger, sickness, loss of children, and loss of parents—they were now heading for the land of Israel.

But there were other problems, too. Before they boarded the ship, a young boy had left camp to purchase commodities on the black market in the nearby village. Yossi heard about it as the boy was being punished by his friends with a beating. He came running and grabbed the boy. Patiently, though angry, he explained to him how the whole operation might have been jeopardized. He told him this was an underground operation that demanded appropriate discipline from everyone and that he had endangered the lives of everyone. The youngsters were angry at Yossi for preventing them from carrying out the boy's "sentence." They said that only corporal punishment could deter such people. But Yossi already knew no punishment would equal the existing humiliation this boy felt.

As they approached the ship, the refugees fell into roll call, and the commanders of the ship reviewed them as in a muster, striding past them slowly, inspecting them carefully. These were what was left of those human beings whom the Germans prided themselves on transporting in exactly forty-five minutes from the trains directly to the smokestacks.

Years later, when Yossi studied naval architecture at MIT, he retroactively calculated the physical modifications of the *President Warfield*, the first large ship acquired in America, which in hindsight was little more than a big tub. From a physical standpoint, the *President Warfield* was liable to sink even before it set sail. By the book, a ship laden with human cargo of such dynamic proportions would have to capsize. To this day Yossi does not know how these ships did not sink into the depths. He remembered how the *Knesset Israel* and the *Exodus*, as well as the other boats, always listed to one side, almost rolling over.

If that was so, why didn't they roll over? After a while, he concluded that just as there was no explanation for the British effort to starve a famished people whose only crime was that they wanted a home, so there was no scientific answer to satisfy the mind for the problem of the weight of these ships. Apparently a strong will could overcome the laws of physics. Apparently human will was metaphysically stronger than all the laws of science. The twenty-five-degree tilt that was typical of these ships was more dangerous than the entire war conducted against them by the British navy. It took daring, naiveté, and above all faith to transport a ship like this with 4,515 people on it, to know the risk involved, and at the same time to remain confident that the ship would make it.

The construction of the bunk levels was completed literally a few hours before embarkation, and the problem of traffic and transportation through the passageways was solved. Here, the problem was different from that of the *Knesset Israel*. The passageways were narrower but less steep. Yossi mulled over what he had seen as a boy in the Arab neighborhoods near the Old City: Arab women carrying huge pitchers on their heads all the way up the mountain, or bringing merchandise to his father's grocery store. Along with the crew, he put in place a system linking the kitchens with the decks that followed the old Jerusalem-Arab tradition of using poles for carrying buckets.

They were supposed to depart at eight o'clock in the morning on July 10, 1947. But the snags on the roads, the limited visibility at night, the delayed arrival of the trucks, the collapse of beds on one of the five decks, and the fact that, in addition, at ten o'clock in the morning a British reconnaissance plane was already circling over the ship, all combined into one great frustration and worrisome warping of their timetable.

Chapter Fifteen

In order to avoid congestion and forestall any glitches, people were transported at intervals. The trucks kept coming, one after another, and the embarkation was completed only toward noon. The harbor police scrupulously checked each passenger. The British did not lessen their pressure, which led to quite a few problems with the French police, who discovered with uncharacteristic efficiency discrepancies between the documents and their bearers.

Each refugee was assigned a spot and allotted a ration of water and food for the first day aboard ship. At a ceremony as festive as could be, while dressed in the finest khaki clothes they had, Yossi and his comrades greeted the refugees. One bundle per person was all that the refugees were allowed to bring aboard. In coming to terms with this, some with silent tears, some with outright fury, people were forced to part with belongings that were precious to them—their sole possessions on earth—while Shmuel Roseman, the chairman of the refugee committee, emotionally proclaimed with a sense of national and personal mission: "Today we are boarding the ship, the ship that is the battle of the Jewish people for its existence."

British bombers were visible circling overhead. The French authorities suddenly reneged on their promise and rescinded the ship's exit permit. With 4,515 refugees and crew members on its deck, the *President Warfield* sat in Port Sète at the mercy of the authorities. Then Yossi gave the order to burn all the documents and Colombian visas and proclaimed with typical simplicity and calmness: "These people have no citizenship, they have no documents, they have no country of origin. Nobody leaves the ship."

The order to block the departure remained in force. The harbor commander instructed Yossi to bring the ship into the bay alongside the docks where there was a revolving gate, with the intent to lock them inside. Yossi refused and emphatically demanded to meet with the district governor. He went with Ike Aharonowitz and Roseman to the governor, and the three of them clarified for him all the reasons they had to set sail at once and that the French had to stop making problems "because blood will flow here." They spoke about the babies, they spoke about the limited supply of fuel, they exaggerated in their account the infectious diseases that would break out, and as an additional persuasive measure they treated the governor and his officials to a gourmet meal with expensive wine. The governor, who looked alarmed and clearly fearful of bloodshed, pledged his assistance.

However, the harbor manager declared that the ship had no permission to set sail, and in order to prevent it from doing so, he was going to dismantle part of the motor and disable the ship. On his way back, Yossi repeated to himself that his artillery was the eyes of the children. Soon thereafter he was summoned for an urgent meeting by Shmariah Zamereth, who had become aware that two British destroyers were already lying in wait for them outside the port in order to escort them.

He went inside and stood by the telephone, waiting for it to ring. Shaul Avigur was on the line and informed him that the British foreign minister, Ernest Bevin, was expected to arrive that day in Paris to meet with his French colleague as part of a series of pressures designed to prevent, at all cost, any waves of immigration. Avigur added that Bevin put the weight of his honor and the honor of Britain on halting the ship's departure. "He's furious, he's cursing. He's possessed," said Shaul. "It's his mission to halt immigration and teach these Jews a lesson. He sees it as a matter of high national security." Shaul went on to say that Bevin had concocted a theory that immigration was a financial conspiracy of the rich Jews of New York, a malicious American Jewish plan designed to make them a fortune. "But," added Shaul, "my assistant just returned from a meeting with the French minister of labor, Daniel Meir, and they managed to come to an agreement. It's unambiguous and final. By morning, you must leave the French port no matter what. Otherwise they will detain you, the operation will be done in for good, and it won't be possible to do anything about it."

Yossi pacified Shaul, saying that whatever a human being could do, he would do. Having checked the harbor himself, Yossi understood all the elements of the situation and asked the pilot to come at once. It was clear to Yossi that none of them knew the maze of the harbor or how to exit the port without the pilot's guidance. Indeed, the pilot was willing, for a very considerable sum, to execute the intricate departure from the port, but only in the dark. He was supposed to arrive no later than eleven at night. Subsequently they were notified he would arrive at two in the morning. At this point, with Shaul Avigur's consent, the command was prepared to triple the sum to a million francs.

By order of the authorities, two French customs officers remained aboard the ship, but the Protestant minister John Grauel treated them to whiskey. By midnight they were in a happy mood, at which point Grauel handed them a few more bottles and sent them on their merry, warmhearted way. Now it was already two in the morning, and the pilot still had not come. Berny, the first officer, released the ropes. They continued waiting, but in vain. At three in the morning fishing boats began to leave port. Yossi was furious. The entire operation now hung on a thread. It was necessary to make a bold decision. He instructed Ike to set sail at once, with or without a pilot. Ike objected, claiming it was impossible. He said he wasn't a pilot, he wasn't familiar with Port Sète, which was actually a port for fishing boats, and added that he refused to take upon himself such a responsibility. He recommended they wait a bit more. Yossi agreed. They waited. Day broke, and the pilot hadn't arrived.

Now Yossi declared that he took full responsibility upon himself and instructed Ike, "Do what you can, you're not responsible, I'll be responsible for the disgrace."

Immediately afterward the engines started up, but the propeller stuck in the shallow water, and the ship came to a halt. One of the American volunteers dove down to check. Upon his return, he explained that when the 4,515 refugees came aboard, the ship settled and the propeller got tangled in the cables. Yossi glanced at his watch. Shaul's words echoed in his head. He knew they had to leave, no matter what. The mechanics tried restarting the engine. They lunged the ship forward and back, again and again, in order to free the propeller, while Yossi stood and waited for them to accomplish the impossible and push beyond the red line. The miracle they were hoping for happened—the cable snapped, and the ship moved forward.

In Port Sète there were half a dozen docks situated at various angles all the way to the exit. The ship sailed without a pilot, knocking and banging into each and every dock without exception. The refugees woke up, not understanding what was going on, but maintained perfect order and calm. Beyond the docks there remained two breakwaters, and in between them gaped the port's opening. In order to exit, they had to make a wide swing to the left. Ike commanded, "Turn the wheel all the way to the left," but in the confusion the helmsman turned to the right, and the ship ran aground on the sandbank, shook, and got stuck.

It was already morning, full light. On the shore sat Shmariah Zamereth with his men, looking at the grounded ship. Immediately they called Shaul in Paris to notify him that the ship left but had run aground on a sandbank. For Shaul it was like Tisha Ba'av, a day of public mourning. He had spent weeks and months painstakingly planning this operation, and now it was backfiring. But Yossi considered his decision to leave the port, after so many stumbling blocks along the way, precisely his most successful, well-conceived act; and after such a monumental victory, how could he just shrug his shoulders and calmly accept defeat?

Instead of despairing—after all, he knew the dire consequences—he gave the instructions for the next step: that the workers make one last effort. Once again they started the engine full force, beyond the red line. The ship moved forward and back, as though it could chisel through a sea of concrete. And very slowly, at distinct risk of endangering the motor, they managed to plow through the sandbank, centimeter by centimeter. For almost three-quarters of an hour the mechanics tried everything. With 115 turns a minute, it became a severe, desperate struggle against the laws of mechanics. A matter of life and death, since at any moment the ship might explode, sending 4,515 refugees to the depths.

After an hour and a half or so the ship glided out of the port. As soon as they entered the open sea, they shut the motors and went down below to check for any damage to the hull or the sides of the ship. Azriel Enav, who operated the wireless, succeeded in contacting Paris through the Tel Aviv–Rome line, and his message got relayed to Shaul Avigur in Paris. They all waited— Micha Perry in charge of the refugees, Zvi Katznelson in charge of supplies, and Sima Schmuckler, a nurse in the infirmary. The entire staff of the ship waited.

Yossi was informed that Shaul sat stunned in uncertainty, staring at the wall, pale as a corpse. He could not believe the cable was correct, after the previous cable that reported the ship had run aground on a sandbank. A few minutes later he was the happiest of men—though, as was his wont, he didn't let anyone see how he felt.

The ship now sailed the high seas and immediately encountered, as expected, the two British destroyers waiting for them. But there were no hitches. It was the first time the British had attempted a blockade on the European coast and also the first time the Aliyah Beth had broken through.

Chapter Sixteen

The *President Warfield* was equipped with good radio transmitters. It was summer. The sea was calm. Right after departure, the refugee committee, led by Samuel Roizman, who had also helped fit the ship, began to operate. Notices circulated for all sorts of classes from Schopenhauer to Hebrew language lessons. Musicians played intermittently on two decks and there were evenings of community singing. The youngsters put on pageants and also practiced military drills.

There was also a love story.

That same young girl who had traveled on trolleys for a year, spoke German, and had been raped near Munich met a boy on the first day of the voyage. He was pale, twenty years old, and always had a pad and pencil in his hand for sketching.

When he discovered the girl, he stared at her at length and suddenly said, "I know your eyes, you're the one who signaled to me from the trolley and warned me about the coming danger."

The girl, who would call herself Aliza upon settling in Israel, said, "Yes, and you have beautiful eyes."

When Yossi passed by, they hushed. Then she asked to see his drawings. The boy, who would call himself Yosef, told her they weren't good enough. Aliza gazed at them and said he had talent but his sketches were too sad. He said he no longer knew how to laugh. She said she had forgotten, too, but had learned.

Two days later they met again. The ship lurched a bit as the sea grew choppy. He was walking on the deck, looking for her, and found her sitting at the entrance to the partition, reading.

They drew close together. They gazed at one another for a long while. Then she asked him if he had a girlfriend. He told her he did but that the girl had died. Aliza was jealous and said she didn't have a boyfriend, alive or dead. The boy sketched her. She combed his hair and told him how the Jews on the trains learned the principle of perpetual motion—they were starving but consumed by lice, so the lice ate them and they ate the lice. The boy smiled.

She said she now remembered him from the trolley window, because he was carrying a bicycle seat and was smiling then. He was surprised about the smile and explained that he used to put small children on the bike's saddle so they could reach the top of the ghetto wall and exchange gold for bread with the boys who came to barter from the Aryan side. Aliza told him he was charming, but if he was betrothed to a deceased woman, her own love for him couldn't compete against her. He said time healed all things.

There was a woman named Esther R. on the ship, an acting teacher, who saw what was going on between the two of them. She included them in her theater. Yosef painted stage sets for her production of *The Dybbuk*, and Aliza played Leahleh, the main character.

Esther tried to persuade the boy to part from his dead fiancée. The two women would sing and laugh, though there was nothing really to laugh about; they simply turned the pain into a laughing matter. They made fun of hell. Later, in Israel, people could not understand such humor. The Holocaust would turn into a sacred myth rife with rhetoric, and it became a sin against the lethal horror to joke about your own death. Both women decided to teach the boy how to laugh. Since Esther was an expert at facial expressions, he learned to laugh with just his mouth at first. Not for real. In the end, he nearly laughed. Then he also realized he loved the girl who would later be called Aliza.

The crew managed to pick up the news from the BBC, which was instantly translated into half a dozen languages and circulated in the form of a seminewspaper issued by the refugees themselves. When they reached Malta, the British escort increased to four destroyers. Every day another destroyer was added.

On the ship, life continued as usual—so usual that demands from the religious Jews escalated. Naturally Yossi did not interfere with their prayers on the decks, but he could not accept their demands for a kosher kitchen and for no cooking on the Sabbath. He thought they would all gather together to pray, and peace would prevail among them. But that was not what happened; they split up into separate groups. As he learned at school in Jerusalem, they prayed the way Jews in the temple did, standing crammed together, each person within his own space. Yossi asked them if each group had a separate God, and they looked at him in astonishment mixed with pity. So prayer remained an exclusive and sometimes hostile act, and even here on the boat the struggle among the Hasidim themselves, or between the Hasidim and the *misnagdim*, their opponents, and between the regular Orthodox and the ultra-Orthodox, did not subside.

Some people who came on deck to breathe pure air got dizzy and felt sick. There were those who wept and those who tried to rejoice. They came in turns, they showered, ate on the top deck, and drank water. They stood in endless lines at the lavatories, and the sick received treatment from doctors found among the refugees.

Aliza was one of the founders of the library. People brought the books they had dragged—along with their few belongings—throughout their journeys and now lent them to the library for the public to read. And there were those who wrote. Her beloved, which was what she called her new friend, continued to sketch, but his drawings became more open, less morose. He wrote to himself: "I saw a German behead my mother with an ax. I think her blood has stopped penetrating my drawings." She was happy for him and asked when he would no longer consider himself betrothed. He kissed her and ran below. She stood at the entrance to the library and wept.

Political and literary debates were held that turned into shouting matches. A tense, bitter "trial" was conducted by a group of boys and girls who argued on the subject "The Value of Cynicism." They debated over the rebellion without a cause described in Turgenev's *Rodin*. They weighed whether suicide was an ideal choice. On the deck of the vessel which they often called "their Auschwitz at sea," ideas were advanced supporting the superior worth of nihilism. They eagerly debated the merits of ethics versus etiquette, which—so explained the sweating, excited speakers—was a matter of personal choice, contrary to ethics, which was the basic foundation for all human beings living together. They debated the concept of historical necessity versus the influence of personality in history as presented by Plechanov in his book *On Personality in History*, which the Marxists among them cited with fervor. Did man make history, or did history make man? This dilemma fascinated Yossi, for in many ways it defined his very essence.

Yossi was spellbound by this ship of moribund creatures bursting with life. A young intellectual who would yell out the number on his arm whenever he was asked for his name, claiming he was at bottom just a number and his birth name had been taken away forever, quoted Anatole France, who said that in Paris there was absolute equality—rich and poor alike could sleep under a bridge—and he laughed as if they were sitting at a café in Saint-Germain on an enchanted spring evening, sipping cognac and discussing life.

A woman who lay on the ship longing for death, her legs that had crossed Europe turned to stone, sobbed: "Tell me, my Hebrew Amnon . . . what will happen to us? Do we have any future at all? Can burnt souls have a future? How can souls made of dust be stitched together? How can one leave as Icarus and return as the Sphinx? What does the eagle in the Hebrew desert look like? Will it be able to distinguish between the number on the arm and the number on the heart?"

On the third day of the voyage one of the pregnant refugees collapsed. They laid her on a board and spread a sheet over her, and two doctors attended her. She gave birth to a son but hemorrhaged and died the next day. Yossi buried her at sea—as he had buried the infant on the *Knesset Israel*. He and the American minister Grauel eulogized her, and Yossi said that when the Jews left Egypt they buried their dead in the desert but continued on their way. They wrapped her body in canvas and a flag, tied her to the chains of the anchor, and slid her into the water. Someone said kaddish. The woman's death was particularly difficult to accept because she died at the gates of Palestine; in Palestine, the other passengers said, she wouldn't have had to die. Those who for so many years had witnessed only death yet still continued to move forward felt for the first time responsible for someone's death. She was their victim, they said. At the burial ceremony many people were allowed to come on deck. Throughout the entire ceremony her husband stood supported by two sailors and wept. After that inferno, the death of his wife was still something impossible to comprehend. "Palestine," he said, "is right here, in the middle of the sea, this is Palestine. Why now?"

They religiously fed the baby, who remained alive after the death of his mother, and in great quantity. There was no milk, so they gave him pineapple juice. A woman of about sixty volunteered to keep him close to her breast, but nothing helped. The baby lived for only three months and died later in Haifa.

Chapter Seventeen

Judging by their extensive preparations and how closely their ponderous warships sailed to the *Knesset Israel*, Yossi knew that the British expected a battle. Though he had faith in the skillful American crew aboard ship, he was disheartened to see that six British destroyers accompanied the ship, sailing on all sides at a distance of one naval mile. Their ships were modern, mostly of the model C type, with long-range cannons on their decks. Alongside the *Exodus*, these gargantuan ships looked like giants closing in on a dwarf. Yossi ordered not to exceed a speed of 11 to 11.5 knots, hoping the British would not discover its maximum of 18 to 19 knots, which he kept in reserve for the final push.

However, there was one detail he did not know then. Every seaman on the British destroyers trailing them had an exact blueprint of the ship and knew where every item was located and precisely what speed the ship could reach. The *President Warfield* had been leased in 1942 for a voyage said to be its swan song, but it served for a brief duration in the British army, transporting soldiers through the La Manche Canal, something it could still manage.

Years later, when Yossi was in charge of rehabilitating one of Israeli intelligence's most important units and thus engaging in various unusual matters, his priority was always precise intelligence, however harsh it might be, because the lesson of the lack of information on the *Exodus* always remained before his eyes.

All this time Yossi maintained constant contact with Mossad le-Aliyah Beth. From their cables he realized that in Palestine people were already talking about the ship. They knew that something portentous was coming. Fund drives were conducted, and this greatly disturbed Yossi, because it indicated that the Jews in Palestine knew about the expedition; and if they did, then so did the British, who would of course prefer to attack as far off as possible from the shore. After all, they had already broken the laws of the sea and blockaded the ship on the coast of a foreign state. He knew it would be easier for them to compete against the ship on the open sea rather than closer to the coast, if it should ever happen that large numbers of refugees would try to swim ashore.

In the morning they received a cable from Palestine stating that the name of the ship was now changed to *Exodus from Europe '47*. Like his comrades, Yossi was furious and cabled to Haganah headquarters: "What kind of a name is that? Everyone here objects. People want a stronger name. Perhaps *Jewish Resistance*, or a name that speaks to the refugees themselves. After all, just one ship in the entire Aliyah Beth carried the name of a refugee killed in a clash on the Langev, *The Unknown Refugee*."

The leadership in the *yishuv* categorically refused and instructed Yossi to follow orders. The leadership was trying to moderate the conflict with Britain over illegal immigration and redirect it toward diplomatic channels, so they stubbornly refused to entertain the thought of the provocative name. But it was precisely this rather neutral name, lacking all protest or call to resistance, that stuck and managed to penetrate the conscience of the world. The *Exodus* turned into a symbol. Only the English continued—and still continue—to call the ship *President Warfield*, named after the owner of a shipping firm on the Potomac, whose niece caused King Edward VIII to abdicate the throne, since he preferred to marry her. His brother, the future George VI, took his royal place. Yossi found it amusing that in spite of everything a touch of royalty adhered to the ship.

Aliza and Yosef, the young pair who met on the ship, he with his painting pad and she with her pain, sat down in a corner somewhere, and the boy conducted a sort of ceremony to divorce himself from his dead fiancée. An old woman handed him a candy she'd hidden in the hem of her dress. Two men from the boy's hometown city of Vilna vacated their palace of twice fifty centimeters, and the new pair shyly entered the lair. A neighbor stretched a string around it and hung socks and a shirt to enclose the space. That was how they became betrothed. Afterward, he tossed his portfolio of paintings into the sea, and from then on until they reached Haifa, and through all the drama that followed, he sketched only her and his mother as a young woman—he remembered she wore a purple satin dress and a ring and kept trying over and over to re-create her figure.

On the ship there was an elderly Ukrainian woman with a bony face who brought along with her two orphans she had rescued and secretly raised in the spirit of the Jewish faith, in spite of the fact that she herself hardly knew the difference between its dos and don'ts. She had barely known the children's parents, though they'd lived near her. The parents had taken the children to her and begged her to save them. The simple, barren woman had accepted this mission, which she'd fulfilled at great cost to her, but not without pride. Out of fear of her neighbors she moved to another locale, because she had more to fear from them than from the Germans. Through all the days of the war she protected the orphans. When hunger raged, she fed them before herself.

Suddenly one of the passengers stood up—one of the many who had lost their children and searched for them in every nook and cranny, in storehouses, monasteries, behind the stove in the kitchen, beyond reason, in agony, one of these Jews who yearned for their dead children, who gazed longingly at the two orphans the woman had raised and cared for, an embittered, childless passenger—and claimed the children were his.

At first many supported him, blinded to logic by their own pain. The woman was shocked and hurt, not just for the real parents, but for herself, too. After all, she loved them. When she protested, they told her, "What right do you have to protest? You're not Jewish," and that pained her even more.

Aliza hugged her and told her with tears in her eyes: "I saw with my own eyes how their parents were taken away to be killed." But the man became angry, insisted, and screamed at her. She fainted, and one of the passengers stood and said he personally knew the parents of the children. Finally, the people who hungered for their children backed off and even brought her a gift of leftover food. When they reached Palestine, these two children became her family. Officially declared their mother, she made arrangements at the cemetery so they could be buried alongside her.

Yossi implemented all the lessons he learned from the *Knesset Israel* on the *Exodus*. Latrine duty was established. Boys distributed toilet paper as needed and scrubbed the primitive privies. The sewage system worked as efficiently as possible, and there was no intolerable stench; everything was fairly clean. Day and night the crew attended to the needs of the community, so most problems got addressed appropriately. Even so, complaints arose, as did grievances and near revolts. But for the most part the situation was under control. The entire community knew beforehand what sorts of conditions to expect en route.

Once they approached Port Said, they began to head north and "scrape" the coast. Early one foggy morning, as they sailed past the mouth of the Nile, Yossi noticed the British ships pulling back. Not one to believe in miracles, he consulted with an officer on deck. They immediately measured the depth of the water and discovered that the *Exodus,* with its flat bottom, could sail closer to the shore than their ships. Secretly familiar with the ship, the British knew this and didn't try to enter the shallow coastal waters where the *Exodus* would have the advantage. They also knew no Jewish commander would be foolish enough to disembark thousands of Jewish refugees in Egypt.

Yossi instructed the helmsman to turn the wheel and sail due north. They sailed from El Arish, north of the Sinai desert, toward Gaza. Needless to say, Yossi and Ike did not trust the British, so they put the crew on alert. Groups of fighters waited in their assigned spots, ready to come on deck with tin cans, steam vents, and the keys for the ropes fastening the huge rafts that, once released, would be thrown into the struggle. The *Exodus* sailed about twenty-five miles from the coast, while the British destroyers sailed all around it, one in front, another behind, and two others between the *Exodus* and the coast. Even before they reached El Arish, in order to test the reaction of the British, Yossi gave the order to come to a full stop.

The ship slowed down, and the British halted. Their huge ships had difficulty stopping, which resulted in a gap that the British quickly closed; the coast of El Arish was not suitable for the disembarkment of 4,515 Jewish refugees, nor was the shore north of the Gaza strip.

From Palestine Yossi received instructions to head farther north and try to disembark the refugees on the coast of Bat Yam. He rejected this option because the coast of Bat Yam was very rocky; the ship was unable to approach the shore any closer than two hundred to three hundred meters, since any sharp turn would run it aground on the sandbank, which would undoubtedly lead to many injuries. Though the Palmach cabled that it would send two battalions to the shore, it wouldn't much matter for those who would already be dead. Finally, it was agreed at headquarters to accept Yossi's assessment that the coast of Tel Aviv was more suitable and practical, and they fixed the location for disembarkment opposite the Kayta-Dan Hotel.

According to the plan, the Palmach would blockade the city for a short while and distract the British with a provocation. But from the ship the Palmach wasn't visble, and neither were the British. Since the cable codes of the *Exodus* were simple, the British easily cracked them and learned the plans, so as soon as the ship left the environs of El Arish they began their attack at sea. Yossi gave the order to cable Palestine. The wireless was able to transmit directly to Tel Aviv, where the Haganah underground could receive radio transmissions from all over Palestine. At headquarters a declaration was prepared. Yossi cabled details about the ship and its passengers and gave a brief account of its voyage, its hardships, and its cargo.

During the transmission on July 18, all traffic stopped in Tel Aviv, in every city of Palestine, in the kibbutzim and settlements. The entire Jewish nation listened. On that same Friday, July 18, far from the territorial waters of Palestine, at two A.M., as the *Exodus* headed north, one of the destroyers drew near, flooded the *Exodus* with the glare of searchlights, and instructed it to come to a halt. As planned in advance, throngs of passengers on the decks fled below. Based on the drills, each of them knew his or her assigned place and task.

The ship did not stop; instead the seamen spun the wheels and turned the ship back out to the open sea. Unfazed, the British began their assault on the high seas rather than risk having to fight against the forces of the Palmach on the shore. They had *Charity, Ajax, Chieftain, Childoro, Chequers,* and *Carigan Bay.* Their detailed battle plan, which had been given beforehand to every commander on the British ships, specified exactly where each ship would stand and the role each would have in the clash. At the signal "Board now," one of the ships suddenly roared ahead and came alongside to attack. With ropes and ladders, the marines tried to surprise them by jumping directly onto the bridge and seizing the ship.

The *President Warfield*'s ability to maneuver made catching it all the more difficult, but it was still a hopeless battle. Five model C destroyers and one cruiser, all of them modern warships in tiptop shape that the British had just now put into service, closed in on a junk heap, ramming it full force. And the junk heap truly trembled, beams collapsed, kitchens shattered, bunk beds crashed, people crouched in congested corners, and His Majesty's sailors stormed again and again. The *Exodus*, though, suited this sort of clash, since it was so tall that some of its decks towered over the decks of the destroyers. But it was ancient and made mostly of wood. At one point three British invaders managed to storm the pilot bridge. The powerful sirens of the destroyers split people's eardrums. The sailors broke through, and by four forty-five in the morning there were already forty armed British fighters on the decks. Some of them got wounded by the youngsters. Some were even grabbed and tossed into the sea. Two destroyers were damaged by the massive ramming, the cascade of barrels and ladders, and the huge rafts unleashed on them.

Bill Bernstein, an American volunteer who had worked on the ship when it was still in the United States, was hit by the butt of a rifle when attacked by a British sailor. He collapsed and died on the spot. His American friends were beaten severely. They lay unconscious or crawled into hiding.

On command, the first three invaders were locked inside the pilot deck, and youngsters previously trained for this purpose tossed crates and flung screws, tin cans, and rotten potatoes at them. The ship continued to head north. The pure air and the view of the sky from the deck infused them with a fighting spirit. The air and the smell of the sea invigorated them. In the course of the battle, they felt renewed strength. So they said. At the height of the assault, the girls stood not far off from them with bowls of water and wet towels in their hands and wiped the blood and sweat from the young fighters.

Ike rushed to the reserve wheelhouse at the stern, broke the pin of the top wheel on the bridge, and from there steered the ship while the three British invaders remained locked inside the bridge without being able to operate the wheels. Now and again they tried to break down the door. They fired shots and tossed smoke screens. But the youngsters who besieged them would not flinch, and Yossi admonished them, "People in the camps fought in order to die with dignity. Here, gentlemen, you are fighting for your lives."

One of the refugees, Heinrich Bauer, who had hidden during the war in a small village near Frankfurt, had learned from the woman who concealed him how to stand on the rooftop and snag the unexploded bombs that landed from American planes and toss them out. Now he taught his friends how to fling into the sea the British bombs that hadn't yet exploded.

The ship danced as the battering did not cease. "This British assault," said Yossi on the loudspeaker so that all the British officers on the ships would hear, "is taking place in international waters. We are not responsible if soldiers are killed. If any do get killed, you are to blame, not us!" Afterward, the Protestant minister Grauel entered the pilothouse. He held a tie in his hand, which he had fashioned out of an American flag. He identified himself and asked the three English seamen to come out. The English, who were indeed wounded, humiliated, and soiled from the rotten potatoes and tin cans hurled at them, refused to obey. So perhaps, thought Yossi, they were simply scared of the wrath of the crowd swarming through the corridors.

The *Exodus* was getting weaker. The battering had damaged it. The destroyers continued to do their work in turns, ramming and receding one after the other. Meanwhile the sailors made additional attempts to take control by means of rafts hoisted in the air with derricks, from which the marines leaped onto the ship's decks. Most of the assaults were repulsed. Any Englishman who wasn't driven back to the destroyers or tossed into the sea got disarmed. Yossi tried to reconquer the pilot bridge. Although Ike did a first-rate job steering the ship from the stern, the bridge was needed for the ship to run efficiently. Nets were spread across the engine room to prevent tear gas grenades from penetrating inside. With the aid of a small military compass, Ike altered the course to northeast. He and Yossi wanted to reach shore as fast as possible, and at all cost. But the British kept up what they were doing. Now there were many wounded, and panic reigned. Children got wounded and fell down, people slipped on the oil poured onto the deck. Many of the injured were bleeding. The wooden sides of the *Exodus* began to split. Enraged and covered in the garbage and black coal dust that had been hurled at them, British seamen who managed to jump with their weapons onto the upper deck fired in all directions and hit the fighting boys as well as the women coming to their aid.

The battle lasted three hours and left the ship wobbling like a drunkard. Soldiers vomited, and water was beginning to seep into the sides of the hull. The second officer reported to Yossi that hundreds would drown because they wouldn't reach the upper deck in time. The responsibility on Yossi's shoulders was enormous; he had two choices—to request a cease-fire or continue the struggle.

At five in the morning the British moved to the decisive stage. The destroyers surrounded the *Exodus* in a closed circle, their prows aimed at it as they danced around, taking turns ramming it full force from all sides. People scampered every which way and hurled whatever came to hand. There were no weapons; Yossi had made sure of that in advance. He conducted the battle with couriers, all the while keeping tight control. More gunshots were heard, and more people got hit by bullets, all told already more than two hundred. Two destroyers on either side of the ship rammed their prows in full fury against the upper wooden structure of the ship. It shook and listed on its side. Marines took advantage of the situation and dropped onto the decks like scores of monkeys from the mast cables of their glorious ships. Yossi gave the order, and *Exodus* turned full speed ahead toward Haifa. The sudden swerve and zigzag of the wheel, which left a tipsy wake, cast a few more British sailors into the sea.

The British strategy and tactics were drafted to the last detail. They can all be found today in the admiralty's portfolio. Meanwhile the condition of the wounded aboard ship worsened. A British officer who saw someone raise an ax against a British soldier shot and claimed self-defense. Oil spilled all over the deck, and smoke spread from the stack. Through the gaping holes in the remaining hold, the stream of water mounted. Yossi and Ike added pails and fortified the groups assigned to quickly and efficiently bail out the water. In all this confusion, Yossi heard a boy's shriek. He ran upstairs only to see that a boy of sixteen, who had served as contact on the deck, had been shot by a soldier standing right by his side, attached by rope to the derrick on his ship. Grauel, the Protestant minister, went and cut the rope with a knife, and the soldier fell into the sea. In the hold of the ship, by the engine room, among hundreds of people in a night of screams, the boy's younger brother labored to bail the flooding waters, but in spite of all his efforts he felt something stir inside him and dashed onto the deck like a madman, to find his dead brother, shot through the forehead.

People scampered like frightened animals and hurled ladders at the hundreds of marines who continued to board the ship in waves. Tel Aviv loomed on the horizon, then Netanyah, as the battle reached its climax. Amid the shouting, they had to turn ninety degrees and head for shore, although Yossi already realized that the Palmach was not waiting for the *Exodus*, and hundreds of British soldiers were waiting instead. He didn't want to endanger the lives of people on the strength of baseless promises. In the authenticated cables he received, there was no mention of the Palmach. But Yossi did have a battered ship, which, in its current condition, was a disaster in the making, likely to cause the death of numerous people. The disembarkment of 4,515 people from that doddering ship would have amounted to mass suicide.

Yossi struggled, therefore, against two forces. He struggled against many of his friends and members of the crew who demanded they continue to fight, no matter how much blood would be spilled. And he struggled against the British, who ratcheted the pressure higher and higher, firing and tossing bombs, boarding the ship and getting repulsed, but boarding again. Only later, from the complaints Ike and his friends lodged against Yossi to the Palmach, did he learn of the audacious suggestion that they hang some of the captured British on the sides of the ship to stop them from battering it. He could only imagine the ferocious reaction of the British had they seen their fighters suspended from the sides of the *Exodus*.

The ship teetered more and more, and people could barely stand on it. At this point there were seventeen British captives.

At nine in the morning, when they were already opposite Kfar Vitkin, Yossi asked to speak with Dr. Yehosha Cohen, the chief doctor on the ship, a wonderful man who was very helpful in Aliyah Beth and whom Yossi trusted. He requested an updated report on the condition of the wounded. Dr. Cohen approached Yossi with bloodstained hands and replied: "If you don't get some plasma for blood transfusions, six or seven will die immediately, and who knows how many more will die after that."

For Yossi, nothing more needed to be said. He had one objective that outweighed all other concerns: to bring them all alive to the promised land. Exhausted but clearheaded, he realized he had a difficult decision, one that was his alone to make. Later on he would reflect, "At that moment I felt like one of the refugees. Even in Palestine nobody would have dared to place the elderly, the women, the children, on the front line of defense. By what authority, and to what purpose, could I ever do this?"

He surveyed what looked like a frightful battlefield, bloody, lost, and so sad. With heavy heart but lucid mind, he gave the order to halt the ship. He approached a captive English officer and asked him to establish contact with the British commander of the fleet to send rations of plasma. And he also asked to report that the deck was flooded with blood. The destroyers now closed in on the *Exodus* like a shoal of bloodthirsty sharks. Yossi didn't stand on his honor. The British High Command received the request, and within minutes a boat was lowered from the British ship carrying a doctor who brought plasma and medicine and began treating the wounded. All the while they continued to move northward—toward Haifa.

Two months later, when the "Jewish wars" commenced and the *yishuv* proved to be divided over how the drama of the *Exodus* played out, Ike would criticize Yossi's decision to stop the battle, calling it a cease-fire. He would also claim that on Friday morning he recommended they try to break loose to Kiryat Chaim. This idea would not have been practical even if Yossi and the commanders had heard it. The choppy sea, the condition of the wounded, the state of the ship, the placement of the British vessels—all this was a guarantee that any disembarkment at Kiryat Chaim would become the scene of a slaughter.

Lieutenant Commander Bailey, the commander of the *Childers*, which led the chase against the *Exodus*, described years later what he witnessed. "*President Warfield* was a phantom vision as it sailed at full speed with all its dead aboard in the dark of night, with two huge Zionist flags waving on the ship's masts, illuminated by our own large searchlights. Her siren wailing in the night sounded like a wounded, lowing cow escaping to hide itself."

Chapter Eighteen

Exodus was the climax in the just struggle of immigration to Palestine. Yossi Harel knew that justice was a complicated word. The orders he gave in battle were circumspect and composed. He addressed people face-to-face, carefully and patiently reviewing every command. He jointly planned the deployment of forces but wouldn't consent to engage in a hopeless battle, wouldn't agree to become the architect of a new Masada, even in the name of a national myth for a resurrected generation. There were those who wished to make political capital on the backs of the refugees, and what they came up against was the wall of a man who knew what hidden power lay in the legacy of heroes fallen on the battlefield for a worthy cause; he refused to sacrifice the surviving remnant of the Jewish people on the altar of this myth. For that reason, too, perhaps mainly for that reason, Shaul Avigur—haunted as he was by the *Patria* disaster—relied on him. Avigur skirted the guiding principles of the *yishuv* and gave him full backing during those fateful hours, and afterward as well, believing that the community should be forced to fight for the refugees and not the other way around.

Some of the Palmach men on the ship were torn between loyalty to their commander, Yigal Alon, who stuck to the struggle through thick and thin, and compassion, having faced the eyes of the children that gazed at them day after day. Yossi was also aware that the British tried to create the impression that the Zionists were exploiting the suffering of the refugees for their own purposes. For Yossi and most of the men of Mossad le-Aliyah

Beth, the refugee was not the torchbearer of Zionism. The Zionist movement struggled to grant him sovereignty, even if he was not a Zionist but just a Jewish refugee looking for a home. Zionism, in this view, defined itself not as an ideal, but as a way to save lives. Yossi took every opportunity to emphasize that the command he accepted hadn't been to bring a ship full of corpses to Palestine. "We did everything we could. We fought for as long as it was worth it. A few more butts from the destroyers and the ship would have simply sunk."

Some Palmach commanders were disappointed and later protested to Ben-Gurion against Yossi's excessive restraint, claiming the resistance of the refugees was the final blow against foreign domination, the war of the Jews for their survival. Alon had contended that "we must resist despite the sacrifices."

In the course of the investigation conducted much later, Yossi argued heatedly: "My consideration was very simple. Resistance—yes. And we certainly resisted. I accepted command of the ship in order to bring refugees to Palestine. I didn't accept the command to convert refugees into fighters, and certainly not to take wounded survivors of the Holocaust just so they could die en route from Netanya to Haifa, nor play with their lives over something we already proved. Leaving Europe was itself resistance."

Yossi saw the pale, frightened children dressed like old people. The name of the ship was emblazoned on a large sheet. As the stricken ship entered the port of Haifa, the choir sang—"We've already planted, but haven't harvested yet . . ."

Everyone was drained. Four were dead. Many were wounded, twenty-seven of them requiring immediate hospitalization. The instruction Yossi received was to first disembark all the crew members needed to bring the *Pan York* and the *Pan Crescent*—the next immigration ships already waiting in Europe. He ordered them to prepare caches under the pilot bridge. Hideaways were also arranged for the crew members. Among themselves, they cast lots to determine who would remain and continue with the refugees to Cyprus and who would return home. The lot to serve as escort fell on Micah Perry. Nobody imagined, even in the ugliest scenario, where the deportation ships would ultimately land.

In Haifa, the loading of the three deportation ships began. A stifling atmosphere prevailed. Terrified people jumped into the sea. The British—aboard police boats circling the ship—pummeled the refugees and fired at them with live ammunition. The young pair of lovers sat on the deck, and Aliza pleaded: "My husband is wounded." He was bandaged, and she caressed him. He wept on her account and was struck again by an angry British soldier busy at the moment collecting canned goods.

The British concentrated on loading the refugees onto the deportation ships, which they accomplished with blows and shouting. Women fainted. Children got trampled. Men screamed. All was in vain. People were lowered from the boat roughly and jostled with contempt and force, herded like cattle between two rows of British soldiers armed with bayonets. And all this took place before the eyes of the members of the UNSCOP committee that had been invited by cable from the *Exodus* to come tour the ship in the port of Haifa.

Some argue that this was all merely an act prepared in advance by the leadership of the community for their own honor. Those who make this claim could just as well say what extremist Arabs or Germans occasionally claim: that it was all one big hoax, that the Jews invented the Holocaust, or at least embellished the truth of what did happen, in order to milk money from the world and rob the Arabs of their country. For the committee, there was no need for explanations. The picture was stronger than words.

Adam M. was on the ship when it stood shrouded in tear gas at the port of Haifa on July 18, 1947. A tall man, he had golden hair—today gone white and sparse—and gray intense eyes piercing through his glasses, and a small crease in his lower lip that has stretched over the years.

As the ship approached, the entire city—even the mountain—was covered in mist rising from the sea. Only the dead or severely wounded were privileged to remain in Haifa. Adam M. was neither badly wounded nor dead. He looked at the Carmel ridge, visible through the fog. He saw what he hoped would be his home, and like all the refugees aboard ship, he too wanted to be reborn and start another life, one without nightmares. The soldiers on the ship did not stop their mates from dragging and kicking him into the deportation ship, where, in a pen enveloped in barbed wire, he lay on the cold iron floor. After three agonizing months of endless wandering, he found himself on a ship that left him off at Camp Poppendorf near Hamburg, Germany.

He had been born in Hamburg. But Hamburg was also the city in which they had shaved his head, stoned him, expelled him, and killed his father. In the past he had loved the city, loved its elegant houses. In his boyhood he had loved the smell of the booty from the North Sea that the boats carried into the port; the mish-mash of languages that he heard at the entrance to murky bars; the dolled-up young women who gave him candies; the bluish northern light of a summer evening; and the cold wind that blew in from the lakes and the sea.

Now he was incarcerated in the British Camp Poppendorf, a former Nazi prison camp converted into a concentration camp for Jews, near the forests where, in another world, after a crystal night, he had secretly learned Hebrew in the *Bonim* movement he'd joined. There he fell in love with a girl whose name he forgot, but he always remembered how she led him into a clearing in the woods, her bashful eyes averted from him, her hair cropped, and then all of a sudden she vanished.

Indeed some of his memories were sweeter, but Hamburg would always remain defiled for him.

After a year and a half in Camp Poppendorf, Adam M. was released and returned by truck to Hamburg. From there, via

Sweden, he reached Haifa, the city he had once glimpsed for one fleeting moment. The refugees who preceded him were already peddling their wares, including cigarettes, on King's Way. He began teaching in a youth club housed in an Arab dwelling whose inhabitants had fled under duress to Wadi Rushmiyah. There he met Hedva, a fellow instructor. They decided to get married and moved to Petach Tikva. Adam M. recommenced his studies. He had to make up for almost ten years of absence from the Polytechnic in Hamburg. They had two sons and a daughter.

On the night between October 15 and 16, 1973, the two sons were killed in the Sinai desert inside one tank. Adam M. searched for their bodies in the desert for many days. He searched by himself, scorched by the sun and wearing a straw hat, his face a closed book. He did not shed a tear, and he did not give up—those who came on the *Exodus,* he said, learned not to give up. In the end he found the tank. The bodies were charred beyond recognition, and only from the teeth, which he brought to a doctor, did he learn the remains were those of his sons. His young daughter died from leukemia, and his wife, Hedva, unable to hold out any longer, died from grief.

Adam M. buried them all one after another, Job with a German accent in glasses, with thin white hair scattered by the wind. Adam M. wrote then that he was the fourth fatality of *Exodus* and that until now he had lived for the others who died. In two handwritten pages he described the hilly landscape of Carmel as he saw it for one brief moment on July 18, 1947. He wrote that if he had died there on the *Exodus,* as was fitting, his children would not now be dead.

Once the *Exodus* was already emptied of its refugees, Yossi and his comrades came out from the caches. Dressed in the longshoremen's outfits of the building company Solel-Boneh, and armed with documents that temporarily permitted them to work at the port, they escaped from right under the noses of the British, on their way to their next mission.

Immediately after Yossi and Azriel Enav, the chief radio operator, met with members of their families in Tel Aviv, they went to meet Yitzhak Sadeh. They reported to him about the voyage and the battle. Shaul Avigur wired from Paris that the ships had disappeared, nobody knew where they were sailing, and they hadn't reached Cyprus. The group was petrified. Three days passed before they learned from His Majesty's government that it was decided to return the refugees to their port of origin. The foreign minister in Vienna demanded revenge. He wanted to teach the French government a lesson for permitting the ship to depart from its territory. But that wasn't the only reason. The British commander of this battle admitted years later that the British empire acted in accordance with its pledges to the Arabs. Another British document excuses the intolerable conditions on the deportation ship, saying that the condition on the illegal immigration ships was even worse. Naturally they did not mention that most of the space on the deportation ships was for the jailers, and the only sleeping quarters remaining for the refugees was one large hall, congested and stifling.

An examination of British sources shows that they prayed for a plague to break out on the deportation ships, or at least one of them, so the Jews would be forced to disembark in France.

Shaul sent a cable to Yossi in Tel Aviv asking how many people in his estimate would leave the ships upon arrival in France. Yossi replied that he suspected more than 85 percent would remain aboard the ships. In reality just one elderly couple went ashore, while all the rest remained. The *Exodus* affair did not end like this. Stuck between the political pincers of the struggle between France and Britain, the refugees decided not to disembark in France. On the *Empire Rival* and two other deportation ships, the beaten refugees danced and destroyed the ships. The soldiers circulated among the Jews with their guns at the ready, cursing. The songs and the dancing drove them crazy, much like those Jewish girls from Germany that Sir John Shaw, the secretary to the British Mandate government, had seen on that scorching day in the Jordan valley. The refugees were sailing on floating concentration camps, suffering from the blazing summer heat in the bowels of the ship opposite the French coast—eating their rations, getting sick, permeated with anger, lusting for revenge.

In an operation ironically called Operation Mae West—after the legendary American actress whose name graced the life preservers worn by airmen—the refugees were transported on Bevin's orders to the port of Hamburg despite strong opposition lasting several days and were disembarked in Germany. So the unfortunate debilitated refugees, after a voyage of two long months at sea under unbearable physical conditions, shuttling between hope and despair, again found themselves before German guards armed with clubs and rifles—humiliated and reduced to dust.

His Majesty's plan was to ship them to the camp during the night to conceal the disgrace, but the refugees fought and objected. Thanks to that, the disembarkment happened in the light of day before the eyes of American newspaper photographers. The fact that the photographs seemed neither to shock nor to stir anyone in the world astonished and strengthened not just the British.

As their next step, the British intended to "return" them, one by one, to their places of birth. The refugees objected to this, too, and when the roster was being drawn up, they gave themselves names like Greta Garbo, Errol Flynn, Hermann Attlee, Adolph Bevin. When asked where they came from, each answered some variation of "My name is Ahad Ha'am,* I was swimming in the sea in Haifa, the British came and kidnapped me." And when the interpreter called them to muster, he would add in Yiddish: "Say no with a capital N."

Ahad ha'am means "one of the people."

A fast was declared. It was publicized throughout the world. Indeed, mayhem resulted—but not in the manner anticipated by the refugees. Only Jews partook of the fast. English and American spiritual leaders remained silent. The religious kept quiet. Izzy Stone, an American journalist who didn't remain silent and had participated in the sea voyage, related that during the disembarkment, which lasted two days, the English played German marching songs.

Slowly, despite everything, the story seeped into the conscience of people all over the world. The name *Exodus* acquired a face.

The concentration of Jews in a German camp began to make waves.

After a delay of several months in northern Germany, the Haganah kept its promise, and the refugees of *Exodus* reached Palestine. Some came with legal certificates. Some came in the framework of what was called Aliyah Daleth, i.e. they arrived with forged documents. The land where Camp Poppendorf was located was where they had begun their journey years earlier, and it was where they also completed it.

Chapter Nineteen

After the clash aboard the *Exodus* in July 1947, Yossi Harel left Haifa Bay disguised as a stevedore. He did not proceed with the refugees to the British detention camps in Cyprus as he had earlier with the refugees on the *Knesset Israel*, because he was immediately asked to set forth and deliver two other ships awaiting him in Italy. Yossi traveled to Tel Aviv, and from the Central Station he walked to Cafe Kasit for a drink. Later, while he was walking down Ben-Zion Boulevard, he saw that a huge crowd gathered beside the Habimah Theater in a vociferous, heated demonstration. British paratroopers in red berets, the so-called anemones, peered warily through armored turrets, cocking their rifles. In the middle stood a diminutive but fiery Jew, Zalman Shazar, the future third president of the State of Israel, declaiming with his usual ardor.

Shazar was speaking of the *Exodus*, though initially Yossi could not figure out which ship he was talking about. Shazar did not merely utter words, he hurled rocks of rhetoric. The *Exodus* became the Macabees, the ghettoes, Joshua Ben-Nun. That same *Exodus* that Yossi had just left, the pathetic *Exodus*, stricken and stinking from tear gas, suddenly acquired biblical stature. In Shazar's report, Yossi's actions sounded like a profile in courage, a film epic, but he was not so sure he had taken part in such a plot. All of a sudden he grasped that perhaps what he had accomplished in the past few months, and all that transpired—the voyage, the fighting, the cruelty, the pain—possessed a significance far beyond itself. Only now did he realize where he had been, that everything Shazar described had actually taken place. He had acted in accordance with his conscience, in a way that had seemed self-evident; the context of his actions became clear only after Shazar put it in words.

He stood pensive and drained, listening with beating heart to a man whose eyes flowed with tears as he bitterly mourned all the 4,500 refugees he never saw, without knowing how they looked or how they were beaten and humiliated by the British. It was as if they had appointed him their spokesman, as if they screamed from his throat. Yossi felt shaken. So while the survivors of the *Exodus*, without his knowledge, began their journey to Hamburg and from there to Camp Poppendorf, Yossi Harel stood and heard a sublime, epic chronicle of these events; for the first time he confronted the fact that the mission he had considered, until now, to be merely one among dozens of daring projects he participated in, had been transformed before his very eyes into a myth of the rebirth of the Jewish nation.

His first thought was, Comrade Shazar, you dear man on that ship, pitiful people with no idea how to be soldiers fought the War of Independence. Children and Palestine Jews, along with Jewish American volunteers. A boy of sixteen, a concentration camp survivor, got killed. An American volunteer got killed. A woman who survived the death march from Auschwitz got wounded. The absurd sight of that short intense leader reminded Yossi of the fledgling Protestant minister John Grauel, who helped smuggle Bricha agents across the borders. Grauel, whose naiveté endeared him to Yossi, wrote articles about the *Exodus* affair for the American press that nobody wanted to read. He was a righteous man, an old-style Protestant zealot who decided one day, out of deep identification, to escort Jewish refugees through border passes while he carried forged identity papers to get them aboard the *Exodus*. In a forest in northern Italy he found himself in the company of nine religious Jews—he had already put the others on a train. It was the eve of Sabbath, and they wanted to say their prayers. Grauel entered a little church at the edge of the forest and asked the Catholic priest to let them pray inside. The priest consented. So Grauel, the fledgling Protestant minister, and the Jews entered the church. One person said, "But we're just nine, we don't have a quorum." His friend lifted his head, saw the image of Jesus above the altar, and said, "Wasn't he one of us!" Then they all began to pray. Jesus served as the tenth man.

And there, alongside the Habimah Theater, Yossi was accompanied by Grauel, by Musa Dagh, by the girl who sang on the bridge the songs of Rachel and Alterman, and everything blurred—entangled—and for a moment he didn't know whether the prematurely aged girl had become Musa Dagh, or Musa Dagh was now *Feldhure A. 13652.*

Chapter Twenty

Yossi was, and remained all his life, a man of the field. He padlocked his feelings and turned his creativity into exploits. Willy-nilly he had to remain true to himself—worthy of any mission imposed on him.

In their tragic outlook, the heads of the Mossad le-Aliyah Beth accepted reality as it was, if only because they had been dealing with it since 1934. They knew full well the phenomenon described and labeled in American historian David Wyman's *The Abandonment of the Jews.*

Yossi was a senior member of the team that fought a war to the death against the sentence passed by the enlightened world against the Jews while the Germans did the dirty work.

In 1938, under the baton of Adolf Eichmann, the Nazis in their Vienna headquarters were still trying to cleanse Europe of Jews by means of transports. But the world did not want them. With the strong support of the Americans, the British put pressure on the European countries, even threatening them, not to allow the Jews sent by Eichmann to enter their borders. Although the death factory—scrupulously crafted at the Wannsee Conference in January 1941—was the culmination of Nazi doctrine, its actual implementation commenced only after there was no longer any place to deport Jews.

When the rescue of twenty thousand Jewish children was discussed in the United States, during a period of great stress in America, an outcry arose against their coming. At that time, President Roosevelt's cousin wrote that these "charming" twenty thousand children would grow up one day and become twenty thousand ugly adults. Immediately afterward, America opened its arms to accept thousands of British Aryan children fleeing the bombing in Britain.

Even in one of the most popular American books about the Second World War, William Manchester's *The Glory and the Dream*, there is no mention of the extermination of the Jews. By contrast, no fewer than five pages are devoted to Frank Sinatra's contribution to the war effort. The deputy minister of the State Department, Breckinridge Long, who was assigned to the problem by the Roosevelt administration, did everything in his power to forestall the rescue of Jews, whether it was by brutal bureaucratic means such as forgery, by shutting his eyes, by slander, or by defining the Jews as a fifth column and a Trojan horse. There was one clear objective—to save as few Jews as possible. A State Department document states openly that if numerous Jews were rescued, it would not be possible to solve the problem of placing them after the war. Another State Department document put it more or less like this: "The possibility that the German government would agree to release a considerable number of Jews in exchange for money or other concessions was a constant worry of ours. Our problem was—what would we do with them?" Such statements were open to only one possible interpretation: the two great democracies, the United States and Great Britain, were, in the words of an official of the American Treasury Department, "deeply committed not to save the Jews."

Conferences like the one in Bermuda were convened with the goal of killing time and prolonging inaction. Pressure from the Jewish lobby led to the establishment in 1944 of a rescue committee, headed by a dynamic man named Pehle. Funding for the committee's activities, particularly for what the Swede Raoul Wallenberg accomplished, came from Jewish organizations. Roosevelt supported the establishment of the committee not out of love for Jews, but because he feared that the outspoken position of the

American foreign minister against saving Jews would be disclosed in the Senate or in the newspapers. The Anglo-American commitment not to save Jews turned into an active campaign and was conducted with the clear knowledge that it had sympathizers. In May 1943 Joseph Goebbels said in reaction to world opinion: "What will be the solution to the Jewish Problem? Whether there will ever rise a Jewish State in some territory is purely speculative. But what is strange to realize is that in those lands where public opinion tends to support the Jews, they refuse to accept them from us. They call them pioneers of modern civilization, philosophical geniuses, artists and inventors, but when someone comes and wants to take these geniuses into their jurisdiction, they seal their borders and say, *No, no! We don't want them!* This is the only time in history, it seems to me, that so many nations have refused to accept geniuses into their borders."

Britain's romantic obligation to the Arabs, who for the most part were pro-Nazi during the war, was more than ideological or financial. They worked against the Jews with fervor. Some sessions of the British government during the war were devoted to the struggle against Jews seeking to flee Nazi occupation. Lord Moyne, the British foreign minister to the Near East situated in Cairo, who was subsequently murdered (in November 1944) by Jewish terrorists, declared that if the British deviated so much as one centimeter from its policy on the deporting of Jewish immigrants, a tidal wave of refugees would flood Palestine. He wrote to the government in London that the Nazis were interested in destabilizing His Majesty's Near East client states by shipping useless Jews there.

When the idea was presented of parachuting food packages into the ghettos where Jews were starving to death, the American government claimed that such an act would violate the order prohibiting any aid whatsoever to enemy citizens. They parachuted food for non-Jewish Poles, who were considered enemies of Germany.

Throughout the war years the United States rarely departed from its anti-Jewish immigration policy. Only after repeated requests that it permit more Jews into its borders, at least during the war, did the administration allow 982 Jews to enter. As the war progressed, in the Reich capital of Berlin, the German underground managed to save an additional 3,000 to 5,000 Jews, in the shadow of headquarters and tight security. In the United States they were considered enemy subjects and were incarcerated in a military camp in Port Ontario in upstate New York. They were forbidden to contact any of their family members and, before being placed in the camp, had to sign a declaration on oath that after the war they would return to what the Americans called "the lands of their birth."

In order to help the Jews, the Jewish organizations asked the United States to accord them the rights of prisoners of war, but even this idea was dismissed out of hand.

In Auschwitz all through 1944, the extermination of the Jews continued at full blast. It was obvious that the war was coming to an end. When the cycle reached the climax of 12,000 people a day, the Germans were confronted with the need to conserve Zyklon B. The Jews were arriving on trains faster than the gas was. Economics professors in Berlin were asked to figure out how to conserve Zyklon B. In the summer of 1944 the life of a Jewish child was not worth two-fifths of an American penny—what it cost in gas to kill him. Therefore, in the wake of economic calculations and considerations, experts came to the conclusion that it was preferable to throw the children into the ovens.

In that same summer, when the British, American, and Russian governments already knew full well what was going on, and everyone was aware of the German death factory, the Americans and English still refused to bomb the gas installations, because the cost of such an undertaking was too high. Wyman describes how when the Americans were asked by the Jewish organizations to bomb the railway tracks to Auschwitz, or at least the railway bridges, they refused, claiming it was difficult for the bombers to reach targets that far away from their bases in England. Only after the war was over did it become clear to everyone that the north Italian region serviced a huge airfield. Swift bombers flew over Auschwitz and attacked the refineries and manufacturing factories near and inside the area of Auschwitz. On Sunday, August 29, 1944, no fewer than 127 Flying Fortresses, escorted by 100 bombers, dropped 1,336 fragmentation bombs—200 kilograms each—on the range of factories around Auschwitz, less than 5 miles from the death camps. The antiaircraft fire used by the Germans was meager and ineffective. On their return, the pilots reported direct hits. When the Buna synthetic rubber factory inside the Auschwitz complex was bombed, the mission was defined as a victory over the enemy in the name of democracy.

But the leaders of the Allied forces said that hitting the extermination facilities would transform the war into a "Jewish war" and would clearly contradict the "objectives of the war." When a few bombs fell by mistake on the camp and killed eighty-nine German SS men, the matter was kept secret and the pilots were reprimanded. Jewish organizations, upon being persuaded by the arguments of the Allied forces that damaging the railway tracks wouldn't accomplish much since it was always possible to repair them, suggested they bomb the gas installations. The Americans were totally opposed, even though the four installations and crematoria were clearly distinguishable in the area; each of them was 340 feet long, and the smokestacks could be seen from a distance. The Allies received the blueprint of the camp from Slovakian inmates who had escaped, and they had plenty of aerial photographs. Auschwitz-Birkenau and its environs got bombed from the air in order to help the Soviet forces advance into Hungary. They bombed the railways tracks heading east, but the tracks heading north, upon which twelve thousand Hungarian Jews were being transported daily to Auschwitz, they wouldn't agree to bomb.

In the fall of 1944 Jewish women working at the ammunition factory inside Auschwitz managed to smuggle explosive material to members of the underground in the camp. The material was handed over to inmates working in the area of the gas chambers and crematoria. On October 7, in an uprising that translated into suicide, they bombed one of the crematoria. The Jewish women who worked at the ammunition factory inside Auschwitz managed to accomplish what the powerful forces of the Allies wouldn't dare attempt.*

During the years 1943–1944, active years for the Mossad le-Aliyah Beth, the Allies put pressure on neutral governments not to accept Jews into their borders, claiming they were enemy subjects and this would alter their status of neutrality. They demanded from their representatives in Switzerland not to leak information about the death factories. After the German army retreated from North Africa, the Americans refused to house Jews in the empty military camps that the Germans left standing near Benghazi and Tobruk in Libya, thinking that if they permitted the Jews to be saved, they would be responsible for the fate of the survivors after the war. Hundreds of Liberty ships hastily built in forty-eight hours with the goal of making one journey—to transport troops, arms, and food to the American forces in Europe—returned to their bases empty. The captains asked to use Jews as cheap ballast for the empty ships—after all, several thousand Jews weighed quite a few tons—but even this was categorically rejected by the Americans.

Given their sober outlook, Yossi and the leadership of the Mossad le-Aliyah Beth had no doubts about the ratios of good and evil. The Allies did as they did, period. The men of the Mossad had no illusions. They were interested in only one thing, for which the *Exodus* became its motto and symbol—as long as it was still possible, Jews must be saved. And if we did not save them, nobody else would. They knew that when one was engaged in rescue work, it was forbidden to succumb to emotions, be scared,

*David S. Wyman, *The Abandonment of the Jews: America and the Holocaust, 1941–1945*. New York: Pantheon, 1984.

or play the hero. Levi Eshkol, the future prime minister of Israel, once said that Israel must be like that "schlemiel" Samson. The hero with long hair, courage, and misery.

"We are too small to be small, and weak enough to be strong."

Exodus was a dilapidated junk heap that, with the pride of paupers, carried on its decks a huge smokestack, as though its passengers had decided retroactively to bring along one of the chimneys from their extermination as a symbol, a legend, an actual artifact for those still remembering the other planet that they had survived.

What preoccupied the rescuers at that time was how to assemble all these human shards on the deck of one ship and announce with flair that a concert, Beethoven's Fifth, would take place that evening and please come nicely dressed.

Wonder of wonders, the Jews bestirred themselves from their enclosures of half a meter by ninety centimeters and washed, brushed their teeth, combed their hair in front of the small mirrors they held for each other, and came on deck to greet the Sabbath, their faces aglow.

Chapter Twenty-one

After *Exodus*, Yossi left on Shaul Avigur's orders for his next mission—bringing the two largest ships in the history of illegal immigration. The ships, purchased in America by Ze'ev Schind, were originally intended to transport bananas. Each weighed 6,000 tons, whereas the *Exodus* weighed 1,800 tons.

The *Pan*s were in good condition and could reach quite a high speed. Each of them was expected to carry about 6,000 refugees. The *Pan York* arrived first with cargo from America, unloaded, and anchored at the old port of Marseilles. Before he ever knew he would be its commander, before he even sailed on the *Exodus,* Yossi caught a glimpse of the *Pan York* on his way to get a Niçoise salad with Shmariah Zamereth and was amazed at its size.

Yossi was assigned to transport 15,236 people across the Black Sea, a sea in which thousands of Jewish refugees had drowned in the early thirties and forties. Yossi felt that he was representing these sunken ships. Though at the time he didn't know all the details, he did know about the *Struma*, which carried 769 Jews wanting to emigrate in the early forties. He knew it had been a pathetic tub, that the exit from Port Constantsa had been mined, that the ship's engine was barely functional. During the voyage they had tried to repair it. Under such conditions the ship sailed from Constantsa to the Bosporus, where it was stopped by the Turkish authorities, securely tied to the dock, and confined to quarantine for about ten weeks. The high commissioner in Jerusalem indicated unequivocally that the passengers were not welcome in Palestine. So 769 famished passengers, accompanied by a Bulgarian captain who was afraid to set sail, attempted to stir up public opinion. As on Musa Dagh they waved sheets on which they wrote, "Help us," and, "SOS," but nobody came. Nobody was dispatched to help them.

The British argued that maybe there were spies among them. From his office in Cairo, Lord Moyne pressured the Turks to send the ship back to the Black Sea. Turkish police clashed with the refugees, shoved them forcibly into the ship's hold, locked them in, then towed the ship to the thickly mined sea. Per Moyne's orders, the *Struma* sailed back to the Black Sea. Without a map it had hardly any chance. The current carried it along, and at a distance of about ten kilometers from shore, opposite the Turkish village of Shile, the ship blew up and sank. Only one passenger, David Stollier, managed to swim ashore. He claimed that if the Turkish authorities had been willing, they could have sent boats and saved a number of people. In the end, though, nobody wanted to mess with the British. The number of those who perished between 1935 and 1945, on that route alone, exceeded 2,400.

What remained engraved in his heart was the story of the *Mefkure*. Yossi would see and experience its very route when he transported Jews one night on the *Pan York* and the *Pan Crescent*, without a navigator, in a sea studded with mines.

The *Mefkure* had been one of three small sister ships, together with the *Morina* and the *Bulbul*. On August 4, 1944, at eight-thirty in the evening, the signal was given for the three ships to set sail from Constantsa.

At the ship's departure for the open sea, German soldiers were photographing the Jews from the pier and bursting into laughter. The hope of leaving was so great, as well as the joy of it, that even if the Jews aboard ship had noticed the laughter, it did not penetrate deeply.

The *Mefkure* had two masts, weighed 120 tons, and was built in 1929. Upon departure from Constantsa, there were around 350 people aboard. It was summer, and a mild summer at that. Many stayed on deck. One primitive latrine served everybody, and there were no faucets for washing and very few pails of water. The atmosphere was like a picnic in hell. Most of the passengers were young. From afar they saw their sister ship, the *Morina*—the faster one—until it disappeared from view. There was constant eye contact with the *Bulbul*, which sailed not far from them. After two days at sea, at one A.M., the ships entered the territorial waters of Bulgaria.

Suddenly rockets sliced the skies, followed by the sounds of explosions. The *Mefkure* shook and listed on its side. Rifle and cannon fire was heard from one end of the sea to the other. The ship, whose engine died immediately, tossed on the waves. A wave, splashed by one of the shells, damaged the electric cable and knocked out the lights. Some of the people jumped into the water in an effort to get aboard the *Bulbul* but were met by a salvo of bullets. The captain of the *Bulbul* blocked the exitways of the passengers and assumed complete control. The captain of the *Mefkure* and its four seamen grabbed the ropes of the single lifeboat and abandoned the ship with all its passengers. Anyone who tried to join them and be rescued was brutally shoved into the sea; the seamen rowed away without looking back. Another explosion and fire broke out, spreading rapidly and burning in its path many passengers and whatever was flammable. After only fifteen minutes the *Mefkure* began to sink. The mast buckled and fell, and a few youngsters on deck who were clinging to each other in terror got crushed to death.

A woman bleeding profusely looked around for a way to escape, but all she saw were two small girls begging with bitter tears, "Help us, break down the door!" But the raging fire caught the coats of the girls, and she was powerless to help them. She jumped into the water and swam toward a naked, bleeding man who was floating on a plank. The waves slammed him hard. She tried to reach the plank, but the man had already drowned, and alongside him floated two others. The plank the woman had sighted got struck by a shower of flashing sparks and began to catch fire. On a submarine that emerged opposite her appeared the Germans who previously had been laughing at the port. She heard one of them shout for joy in German: "The Jews are swimming to Palestine!"

The woman was swept farther and found herself up against a floating door with a few people on it, some of them alive. She grabbed the board and again heard gunshots. She closed her eyes, thinking that her end was near, but then a wave came and separated her from the board, which sank immediately. She was saved, so she thought. Then she saw a huge, menacing dog swimming toward her. Its mouth was open, and it almost snatched her in its jaws. It was breathing heavily. Laughter was heard. The dog laid one paw on her neck. An enormous wave rose and rammed a plank against the dog, crushing its skull. From the strength of the blow, a corpse erupted from the water. She screamed, without knowing why, "You dog! You dog!"

A man floating on a chair fell over. He tried to use a cane to row himself and smacked the head of the dead dog. The woman finally reached the *Bulbul* together with another bleeding man who joined her. But he too now drowned. She tried to get closer to the ship. The captain cursed her, cursed God, cursed his mother, cursed the Jews who sent him, and pushed her off with an oar. A cable caught on fire and sank into the water. As bullets whistled all around her, she whispered: "I don't want to die!"

The bowels of the sea filled with stench, blood, and corpses. A man who seemed familiar to her took off his shoe and wept. He found some planks and tried to make a raft of them but had no rope. He saw two ships signaling in the distance and screamed for help. Nobody came to help them. The water was cold as ice. A dead man tied to a life belt floated nearby, holding a baby. A wave knocked the baby loose, and it fluttered.

The woman reached the *Bulbul*, which was progressing slowly. Some boys who had managed to break the locks and come up from the ship's hold to the deck threatened the captain with drawn daggers and demanded that he save everyone; but there were not many left to save.

Vera, a former champion swimmer of Hungary in her ninth month of pregnancy, pulled her nearsighted husband along with her in the water. The woman she had sighted managed to climb aboard while still holding on to her neck as if the dog were biting into it. As Vera and her bundled-up husband neared the *Bulbul*, a rope was tossed to her, enabling her to reach the deck. After several miserable hours they disembarked, still frightened of drowning, and came to the village of Jenda, where Vera gave birth to her baby.

The sunken *Mefkure* was a casualty of the German submarine and also, it seemed, a torpedo boat called *Salvador*. Yossi, about to sail its route, knew that out of its 350 passengers only 5 were saved: 3 men and 2 women.

Sometime later Sheyke Dan would relate that Yitzhak ben Efraim—his comrade in actions behind enemy lines—had been in Constantsa on the eve of the departure of the three small ships. The pressure on the rescue team had been enormous. The refugees all wanted to leave the smoldering continent.

Yitzhak ben Efraim's parents had not known that he was in the city engaging in underground activities. He was not able to meet them, but he was able to arrange their papers and encourage them to board the ship, and that he did.

When they boarded the *Mefkure,* happy and full of hope, ben Efraim was hiding in the railway station, peering at them through binoculars with pride and love, unaware that he had prepared their papers for their final journey.

The *Struma, Mefkure,* and *Salvador* hovered in Yossi's mind as soon as he began preparing the voyage of the *Pans*.

Because the British shadowed every move of the Aliyah Beth, the *Pans* made two voyages to North Africa carrying merchandise. Gad Hilb, who would later captain the *Pan York*, served as skipper on one of these voyages, in order to familiarize himself with the ship.

There was talk about a huge exodus of Jews from Romania. Half of Romanian Jewry had been exterminated. At the end of the war the situation of the remaining Jews was especially difficult, and although the slaughter had apparently ended, Jews in Romania lived in constant terror. At that time thousands of young Hungarians, after escaping the death marches from Auschwitz, were hiding in Romania with the help of men from the Bricha and the TTG. These refugees constituted the more than 15,236 reasons it was necessary to transport so many people in one sea voyage. The borders of Europe were about to close, even for the men of Aliyah Beth. Political uncertainty prevailed in Romania.

Although Yossi was only a few years older than the young hotheads in the Palmach, Shaul treated him as a man of his generation. After *Exodus* Yossi served as adjutant to the chief of staff, but any request from Shaul Avigur was like an order, so in November 1947 Yossi was released from this post and, along with a small group from Aliyah Beth and Palyam,* set out on a mission armed with a Palestinian passport.

They took a regular flight to Prague, on a South African airline, a flight that in those days consumed almost a whole day. In Prague they stayed at Hotel Metropol, where a Mossad summit conference was taking place, a very rare occasion for them. Shaul Avigur arrived from Paris, Sheyke Dan from Bucharest, and Fino Ginsberg, the secretary, from Geneva, and Ya'akov Salomon, the chief of staff of the Balkan coast, was there, too.

The entire staff sat together and planned the grandest undertaking of Aliyah Beth, which would also constitute the fitting response to Bevin for his share in the *Exodus* affair. They submit-

*Polyam (Ha-Pluga Ha-Yamit): the naval corps of the Palmach.

ted details of the complicated logistics concerning the trains that would transport the refugees to the assembly points, and Shaul reported that the whole enterprise would be under Yossi's command; with two ships involved and thousands of people, there had to be only one commander in the field.

At the end of the discussion, Shaul softened somewhat, changed. Smiling as he never did, he said, "Since Moses led the Exodus from Egypt, there hasn't been a Jewish exodus like this. The immigration of Ezra and Nehemiah was gradual and extended over a long period of time. The *Pans*, which have twice as many passengers as Netanya has residents, will comprise the greatest exodus in Jewish history." And immediately he reflected and came back to himself, embarrassed and flushed by his display of emotion.

Chapter Twenty-two

After the meeting they went directly to the work awaiting them. But for Yossi, an additional clock was ticking. Sheyke Dan, his friend, kept reminding him of the fate of the *Struma* and the *Mefkure*. He wanted Yossi to know what to anticipate.

The thing that weighed on his conscience like a millstone were the eyes of the children he saw staring at him even when they were not around. Wherever he went he remembered the children he would have to bring through a path full of mines and pitfalls.

Yossi was ill at ease and couldn't chase the debacle of the *Struma* from his mind. In a long and difficult conversation with Shaul, he asked for explicit, unequivocal instructions regarding his command and what was required of him. For how long would his command be valid? What would happen if they arrived at Cyprus? Didn't a separate chain of command exist there? Similarly, he requested clear directives concerning resistance against the British if and when there would be a confrontation with their destroyers and cruisers. The aftermath of his encounter with the British on the *Knesset Israel* and the *Exodus,* when everything was improvised and he received conflicting orders from Mossad le-Aliyah Beth and Palmach headquarters, still haunted him. Yossi wanted unambiguous directives, not plausible interpretations. Shaul, in his characteristic manner, answered: "I hear you." But Yossi dared to be persistent and told him, "'This time I hear you.'"

He explained to Shaul that in a confrontation with the British, their destroyers would have difficulty landing marines aboard the *Pan*s on rafts because of the difference in height, which was in favor of the *Pans*. "So we'll trail barbed wire," he elaborated, "to snag the propellers of the British ships if they try to approach us from the rear. And at the same time, we'll extend the cranes outward on both sides of the ships, each crane weighing half a ton, to prevent the British from getting close enough to jump aboard. But even with all these precautions, a problem still exists. These modern, powerful British ships could destroy us just by ramming us with their prows, without even approaching us or landing marines, or having to deal with the cranes defending the sides of our ships. Look," Yossi told Shaul, "the order I got was to resist. I'm a soldier. I follow orders. But I want to hear it from your mouth and not from somebody else's."

Shaul pondered for a few moments and asked, "In the event that . . . how many do you estimate would get injured?"

Yossi replied, "The word is 'killed,' and in my opinion at least twenty or thirty would get killed."

Silence, until Yossi said, "If you order me to resist, I will resist. But think with your conscience, not with your head. This isn't Hanita, there are no trained fighters here. We're talking about refugees who went through a Holocaust and cannot trust their own shadows. About a man who wants to father his dead son with a woman in Givatayim that I brought on the *Knesset Israel*, who told me Palestine is good, woman is good, life is good. Know whom you're talking about. Who but you would understand this . . . our struggle is to bring them to Palestine, not to turn them into soldiers in a lost battle. We have no right to compel them to be the commandos of a state in progress when the state in progress is the home they are in need of. They are without trust and utterly drained from years of wandering and betrayal. We have no right." After a moment of silence he added, "With *Exodus*, the British launched the blockade in Europe. In my opinion, fifteen thousand refugees can break the siege just by making it into the Mediterranean Sea. That passage is in itself the guarantee of reaching Palestine, and that is what victory means. That is precisely our struggle. Every Jew who doesn't get killed is our reward."

Yossi was twenty-eight years old then and felt rather insolent speaking the way he did to Shaul Avigur, a legend in his own lifetime. But he knew that he was right and spoke from deep inner conviction. "The departure itself, and the entrance into the Mediterranean, constitutes the goal. It doesn't matter if we end up in Haifa or Cyprus. After Cyprus, Europe will no longer be an option. There will be only one direction, Palestine."

Shaul gazed at him in tense stillness. The muscles of his face contracted, altogether pulled back, like the jaws of a nervous bulldog. Shaul was cut in stone, but even stone could crack. He appeared sad as he said, "I'm listening." That was a sign for Yossi that the road was open.

Yossi continued. "In my view, resistance is not the main thing, and doesn't serve our purposes. Besides, the British want it! They want to teach us a lesson. So why not show them we can break through their blockade, that the extermination was not final or absolute despite their not insignificant help. Why not show them there are still Jews left? Come, let's not be some last righteous Jew thrown into the sea who screams, 'I was right!' and drowns. What justice is there if you've drowned in the sea you didn't have to drown in? I admit there may be two breaking points. The British, at the Bosporus, may try to do to us what was done to the *Struma*, or what the Germans did to the *Mefkure*, and if they succeed, we lose the battle. Or maybe they'll try it at the Dardanelles. But if we pass these two straits, and I believe we can do it, then from my vantage point the battle is over."

Shaul mulled. He mulled for a long time. And he murmured, "Do so." He didn't explain what he meant by the word *so*. But Yossi knew him well and realized that the decision, however tersely rendered, equaled approval. If he had wanted anything else, he could have substituted Yossi with another man.

Chapter Twenty-three

Sheyke Dan flew to Bucharest to arrange for Romanian visas. Every morning during the nerve-racking wait, he called the Jewish foreign minister, Anna Pauker, whose father he remembered from the *Knesset Israel*. Under British pressure, she gave him the runaround. The situation became progressively worse. It was winter; thousands of people waited at collection points, the ships waited at the ports, and all the while the English waited in ambush. It made no sense to wait any longer, and they decided to leave for Romania with the help of the Bricha men.

Meanwhile *Pan Crescent* set sail for North Africa to deliver merchandise. It was expected to sail from there directly to the destination port in the Black Sea, but problems developed in the engine room, and they were forced to stop again for repairs. Ada Sereni managed to secure a docking permit for the *Pan Crescent* in Venice. While they waited in the dockyard, three Britishers came aboard, representing themselves as tourists, escorted by Italian police sent as it were to protect them. The Englishmen were told the ship was slated to transport sheep from Australia. On deck there was a mound of toilet seats soon to be installed. At the sight of the mound, the Englishmen expressed amazement over why the sheep would need so many toilets.

Meanwhile the ship was repaired in dry dock. On the day that *Pan Crescent* was scheduled to depart, at nine in the morning, a powerful explosion was heard. Now the real purpose of the visit from the "tourists" was clear—British frogmen had attached demolition material to the ship's hull. The plates split open and water began to flood inside.

The ship started to sink. The Italian workers fled for their lives. Luckily the explosion occurred at Venice and not after the embarkation of the refugees at Constantsa. Berchik, the commander of the ship, along with the entire crew, mobilized immediately to work the pumps and bail out the water.

To their relief, the ship was still at harbor where the water was shallow, so when the prow sank, it hit the bottom of the bay and stopped. A short while later the Arab League claimed responsibility for the explosion. Once the ship was lifted onto dry dock for repairs to the plates, it became clear that the damage would delay departure for three more weeks.

When the ship was finally ready to set sail for Rumania, the skipper went to pick up the ship's papers. At the office he was told the papers were missing. Realizing that the British had preceded him there, he declared: "If that's the case, I have a notice for you. I won't move the ship from dry dock, and the owner of the ship will pay for the repairs later on." Just as he knew there was no law against extending one's stay at dry dock, he knew that every day at dry dock cost a fortune. Venice had only one dry dock, and the management knew there were lots of ships waiting to enter, and money was money. Besides, they weren't so sure that somebody would actually pay for the extra time. They had no choice but to return the papers to him.

In time, Ada Sereni learned from the mouth of a confessing priest (apparently only in Catholic Italy, where they didn't take God too seriously, could a priest put Ada Sereni, as impressive as she may have been, above God's commandment) that the person who directed the British frogmen that sabotaged the ship was the Italian skipper, who had left a few days earlier. He told the priest that the British threatened him, and he was forced to show the frogmen the location of the engine.

The British, who anchored a ship nearby named *May Pie*, heard about the plan of the *Pan Crescent* crew to take revenge on them and lodged a complaint with the Italians. The latter, who feared flare-ups in their quiet port, asked the Palestine Jews to refrain from retaliation. In exchange they suggested they would delay the British at dry dock at the time the *Pan Crescent* left port. So when the *Pan Crescent* moved past the British ship next in line for dry dock, they saw its sailors standing at attention and saluting. Berchik exploited the international convention, whereby when a military and a civilian ship cross one another's paths, the civilian ship lowers its flag to half-mast and the military lowers its flag completely and then immediately raises it again. Since the crew must salute at attention whenever the flag is lowered, they were prevented from observing the ship closely enough to identify it.

In the meantime, Yossi and his comrades were waiting for visas in Prague. They had to reach Constantsa without further delay. They possessed documents, but the visas for Romania were still held up, so the Bricha men were forced to improvise. They drove to the Austrian border in their small Mercedes automobile. At every point along the border there were Bricha men situated in one disguise or another. The one at the Czech post telephoned the one at the Austrian post on the other side of the border and said, "I have five Austrian infiltrators captive here, come and get them." The Austrian came and took them, and from there they drove by car to Vienna. The next day the routine was repeated at the Austrian-Hungarian border. Thus did they reach Budapest. But since at every border they had to walk several kilometers between stations and their shoes got worn out, one of the group said he knew an excellent cobbler who could custom-make fabulous high boots for them. And indeed the cobbler showed them superior leather, and in twenty-four hours the boots were ready. But after walking eight kilometers in these new boots, the skin on their feet peeled. In the end many of them walked barefoot.

With their boots slung over their shoulders, they also crossed the border to Romania and took a train to Bucharest, where Sheyke Dan was waiting for them. They immediately began planning the operation. Again the problem of fuel came up. Since the

British controlled the Shell Company, and British intelligence co-owned it, all the ships of the illegal immigration, including the *Pans*, had difficulty locating fuel. They had faced the same problem with the *Exodus*, but two large ships requiring eighty tons of fuel per day created a problem many times more complicated. Sheyke Dan scoured the region in search of fuel sources, but the British barred him wherever he went. Salvation came from an entirely unexpected spot.

It may be that all the exploits of the Aliyah Beth amounted to last-minute lucky breaks or con artistry, along the lines of the talmudic adage "All is determined, but free will is given." In any case, it wasn't an act of God—the God to whom the survivors had called upon so many times during these years. The godless luck was connected to two foreign gods—Stalin and Tito. It just so happened that just as the Bricha men docked the *Pans* in Romania and began hunting desperately for fuel, Tito decided to raise the flag of revolt against the Soviet Union. In turn, an oil train on its way to Belgrade was stopped en route by the Russians, who, on Stalin's order, instructed the train conductors not to deliver the fuel to Yugoslavia.

The Romanians, who suspected Sheyke Dan and were close to being persuaded the British were doing the right thing, decided that the *Pans*, whose presence was already known to everyone, should be sent to Bulgaria. Now, under even more time pressure, a solution was found—Sheyke purchased the entire train with all its contents at the Yugoslavian border, and fuel got delivered to the ship.

No sooner had this problem been solved than a new problem arose that was much more severe. The British Mandate in Palestine was about to expire. The UNSCOP committee had submitted its conclusions, and the resulting recommendation was to partition Palestine into two states, Jewish and Arab. For many reasons this was not the time to make waves by bringing 15,236 refugees and aggravating the political struggle while the leadership used immigration as one of its propaganda weapons.

Shaul and his men, who for months had been plotting their undertaking to the last detail, exhausted themselves over how to bring the *Pan*s to Palestine. They were the only ones who could truly understand and convey to their leaders struggling with the problem in Palestine the impact this bitter news would have on those 15,236 men and women waiting impatiently at train stations and at collection points.

The British were under the impression that this transport was a question of only 6,000 people, and still they pressured the Americans, asking them to link their declared support of the forthcoming UN decision regarding the establishment of a Jewish state alongside an Arab state with a refusal to permit the *Pan*s to depart. Even at this hour, when the British empire was shrinking and the British Mandate in Palestine was about to expire, they took the side of the Arabs. They feared that these "6,000" Jews, some of whom were certainly young, would constitute a military problem for the Arabs, who hoped to win with a crushing immediate invasion set for May 15, for which the British had equipped them very well, even if they apparently did not actually take part in it.

Shaul flew to Palestine to meet with Ben-Gurion, who was on the horns of a dilemma. It was not an easy decision. On the table were humanitarian, political, and diplomatic factors, along with a great desire for harmony. It was clear to him that war would break out very soon, and it was critical that the community be united.

Sheyke Dan reminded Shaul before he left for Palestine that once, during a debate over the immigration of the Jews of Bulgaria, Ben-Gurion told him, "Send ten thousand pairs of shoes," and Sheyke had answered him, "Bring the feet to the shoes, not the shoes to the feet."

Shaul explained to Ben-Gurion that he was bringing more feet to shoes. It was impossible to delay the voyage any longer, and among his attempts at persuasion, he employed—without realizing it—a British argument, saying the immigration of thousands of refugees, not a few of whom were young, would alarm the Arabs and perhaps forestall the war. In the end, Ben-Gurion decided that Shaul and Sheyke should fly to New York for a meeting with Moshe Sharett to persuade him. Sharett had been leading the discussions there on this complicated matter, and he was decisively against the departure of the ship. He was in New York, listening very carefully to the loud voices of the American bureaucrats, and he was very concerned about the fate of the vote at the UN.

In Palestine and in New York, heated debates on the subject proliferated, debates that got reduced with painful cynicism to "ships or state." In the throes of debate, the simple fact was forgotten that the coming of these refugees could not actually cause such a serious problem, whereas their rescue was the heart and soul of Zionism—providing a home for the homeless. Shaul advised the leadership to notify the Americans that the decision to depart was given prior to the UN vote; therefore it was valid and legal. The English on their side drummed into the ears of the Americans that hundreds of Communist agents were hiding on the ships. The American secretary of state, George Marshall, was furious. He openly defied President Truman; he could not conceal his opinion on, and feelings toward, the Jews. He alarmed some of the leaders of the Palestine Jews because he threatened quite unambiguously that the United States would not vote for the establishment of a Jewish state if these ships set sail. Therefore many of the Jewish Palestine leaders tried to prevent the departure. Now Ben-Gurion was not the only one torn; Shaul himself was, too.

Shaul was clearly in favor of the departure, but the American threat proved effective. He was aware that the American-Soviet struggle had commenced, that the cold war was looming, and in turn he realized that the rehabilitation of Germany took precedence over the rehabilitation of the Jewish people. Michael, the king of Romania, had abdicated his throne, and the Communists controlled the country. An old-new spirit swept across Romania, accompanied by expressions of reproach and hatred toward the Jews that continued to escalate. This fact too caused Shaul great distress. When he and Sheyke landed in Paris for an interim stop-over en route to their meeting in New York with Moshe Sharett, they had an alarming telephone conversation with their men in Bucharest. The Romanians had issued an ultimatum: If the Jews didn't leave at once, their permits would be rescinded and the ships would never set sail.

On the spot, Shaul canceled the meeting in New York and remained in Paris. Sheyke flew to Sofia and from there to Burgas, the exit port from Europe, and gave the order to set sail. But the language of the telegram he sent clearly reflected Shaul's struggle with himself. It said: "Go in peace. May it be fulfilled that you *wrestle with God and with man and prevail.*"

In this language Shaul Avigur summed up the tortured turns of his soul. Let the ships depart, may they arrive in safety, perhaps this was nothing but a political blunder. For when one spoke of rescue, politics must come second. But when one spoke of politics, rescue could perhaps wait.

Several days before the departure—in a move Yossi knew nothing about—Shaul arrived at a reluctant compromise by which the ships, if indeed they managed to cross the straits, would sail directly for Cyprus and surrender there. The important thing was that they leave the continent immediately.

There were some in the Zionist leadership who, to support their stand against the bringing of the ships, argued that the Jews of Romania had suffered less than others, since "only" half of them had been exterminated by the Nazis; hence they could wait. This statement was not just dubious from the factual point of view, it was fundamentally vicious. "You cannot measure suffering with a ruler," said Yossi, "danger is not an exact science. Fifty percent is a very high number. After all, one person on its own is a hundred percent! That fifty percent was sent to Bratislava, and thousands of them were murdered with unprecedented brutality. People were hung on hooks in slaughterhouses in the city of Yassi. Many were burned alive in Czernowitz and multitudes were exterminated." In addition to the Romanians waiting to board the ships there were Hungarian refugees, those few who remained alive after the death marches.

The departure orders were ambiguous, but they did specify that the ships should sail without bearing any Hebrew names. Also, the Haganah should not be mentioned in any context. The "British bastards" should be obeyed, but under no circumstances should they return to the Black Sea. They were asked not to resist, but definitely to persist. "You are beyond British jurisdiction," declared the instructions, since Haifa was already in the hands of the Israelis and was a Hebrew port free of the British, "and if problems arise, tell them that you are abiding exactly by the decision of the UN—that because of the nature of the 'transport,' it was impossible to delay the voyage. Avoid provocations. It is a pity to besmirch the name of the Haganah."

And with the same tag gracing the end of every decision, the cable concluded with the motto "Rise and succeed."

Chapter Twenty-four

The orders were fuzzy and full of contradictions. In the end the ships set sail without official authorization, without any reference to the Haganah, but by instruction—itself ambiguous—of the Mossad le-Aliyah Beth. It was clear, though, that Ben-Gurion's silence behind the scenes amounted to endorsement.

Had Yossi or any of his comrades felt for a moment that bringing the *Pan*s would endanger the Jewish community in Palestine or jeopardize the establishment of the state, they would have canceled the departure. The Mossad agents who worked for years to save Jews wanted to rescue the Jews rotting away in Romanian prisons or Communist solitary cells. The Jews of Romania lived under a brutal anti-Semitic regime whose leaders were former Royalists, then Fascists, later Nazis, and now Communists. The Romanian government could be described in the same terms used by the Romanian playwright Eugène Ionesco to describe his father: they changed uniforms the way a woman changes dresses but still remains the same woman.

On the empty deck of *Pan York*, at the final stages of preparation, Yossi and his colleagues waited in the bitter cold, on November 29, 1947, for the decision of the UN assembly. They sat and listened to the radio and, along with the entire Jewish people, counted the votes. The deck was covered in snow, and at the end of the vote they celebrated with drinks but knew that even though the decision was in their favor and the Jews would now officially have a homeland, the British would still be lying in wait for them, eager to fight.

From reports arriving from the field, it was clear that *Pan York* would have the greater number of children, seven hundred under the age of five—orphans of the slaughter in Hungary and Bratislava.

The deployment of people across Romania and Hungary in the snow was the most complicated undertaking in the history of the illegal immigration. The Jews were without trust. A lovely black-haired young girl in a beret, who had emerged from a pile of corpses, had difficulty closing her eyes. The muscles of her eyelids had stiffened. She slept with her eyes open —in frozen amazement. Yossi met her after she boarded the ship and tried to calm her, just so she could learn to shut her eyes. Only after twenty years did she learn to do this. But even then her dreams were dominated by visions of her parents getting slaughtered alongside her, so she went back to sleeping with her eyes open until the day she died.

And what arguments were there in front of a family that emerged from the long death march alive and couldn't understand how it survived! None of the five who had escaped—father, mother, and three children —could understand why they in particular remained alive In the passageways of the ship people asked why they and not others were spared. Nobody had an answer.

The passengers of both ships knew what logic refused to explain. What prevailed "there" was the camaraderie of the condemned. One woman said that Amnon explained to her that what happened "there" was a nightmare and what was about to happen was real life. From then on she tried to accept that she once dreamed a long, evil dream, which she perhaps never really experienced.

There was no going back now, Marshall or no Marshall. Berchik said, "We always pretended we were transporting sheep or cattle or bananas on the immigration ships. This time we're brazenly fitting banana boats for people." Actually, the fact that the ships were designed to carry fruits benefited them. The ventilation system necessary for transporting fruits, mainly bananas, which need air circulation four times a day, generated clean air in the ship's hold. In order to increase the ventilation for human requirements, Berchik consulted the manager of a large movie house in Bucharest, who showed him the system he set up in the huge auditorium. Berchik put this information to use when combining the ship's two ventilation systems. Subsequently this hookup led to glitches in the electrical system, causing some awkwardness and disruption in the passageways. Nevertheless it enabled 7,500 people on each ship to breathe even in the enormous halls below deck that hummed like beehives, with each person confined to his or her own bunk.

It was critical to provide a large amount of drinking water, 150,000–250,000 liters, based on their calculation of 12,000 liters of drinking water per day. They converted the empty space at the prow of the ship into a huge reservoir of water, and to prevent pollution from the rust that would form on the ship's sides, they covered the area with cement.

The shelves in all the sleeping halls were numbered. Although congestion was intense, organization overcame pandemonium. They built 134 lavatories on deck, a ratio of one to sixty.

Based on their accumulated experience on previous ships, they arranged for each ship to have forty-four nurses and twenty-four doctors, all refugees themselves. Each ship would have three infirmaries, including an operation room and a delivery room. For social activities, a library of classical music records was set up. The area of living quarters—home or "property," as some called it—the metric boundaries allocated each person, came to fifty centimeters for the duration of the voyage.

At each of the three stations for water distribution, three faucets were attached. The distribution of food to groups comprising three thousand people would last forty to sixty minutes. It was necessary to factor the amount of time it would take to come on deck and then go back down again and adjust accordingly. It was also necessary to set up lines at water distribution stations, so the distribution would last from twenty-five to thirty-five minutes. They arranged it so that each cycle coming for services, necessities, and water would consist of groups of forty-five, each group with somebody in charge. They would announce on the loudspeakers those appointed, so each group leader would know where to be and when. Once a day the entire passageway from aft to stern would be available for visiting with relatives and breathing fresh air.

In essence, each ship was divided into three ships with separate kitchens and lavatories. Yossi knew that concentrating so many people in so confined a place would create stress and fric tion, and in turn he hoped that walking on deck would constitute relaxation therapy.

While they were still preparing for departure, a British oil tanker arrived at Constantsa to refuel. After the sabotage at the port of Venice, they suspected the real identity of the tanker and feared it was a cover for another sabotage ring. They patroled with boats around the *Pans* while the tanker was at port to make sure there would be no surprises.

The Romanian authorities struggled more and more beneath the pressure of the British, and it was feared they would break. Sheyke Dan had to come up with a creative solution, particularly in light of the Romanian suggestion that the ships set sail for Burgas without the refugees. The deal that Sheyke concocted was convoluted: The ships would leave from a Romanian port without the Jews of Romania being licensed to come aboard. The Mossad would cover the expenses of transporting the Jews by train from Romania to Bulgaria and bribe whomever necessary in exchange for 15,236 visas, which they didn't have. This arrangement provided the governments of Bulgaria and Romania with sufficient cover against any British complaints, if and when they came. Romania could argue that the refugees did not leave from a Romanian port and the ships were simply dispatched from its territory, while the government of Bulgaria could argue that the refugees did not leave from its territory. Thus did the two ships depart completely equipped, but without any refugees aboard, and sail from Constantsa in Romania to Burgas in Bulgaria.

At departure from Constantsa, the sea was stormy. The waves rose to a height of seven meters and crashed with a roar on the bow. A Spanish crew working on *Pan York* comprised excellent, disciplined seamen. And, as one survivor put it, they had heart, they cared. They had come with fresh memories of the Spanish war in which they had been brutally and wickedly defeated by the Fascists. They could identify with the suffering of the Jews.

The crew of *Pan Crescent* was Italian, and some had notified in advance that they would not stay. Actually, the Italian mechanic had already left at the beginning of the voyage, and another mechanic had taken his place. In turn, when the ship began to move backward, he did not know what to do. Berchik dropped anchors and ran the ship aground on a sandbank. The propeller sank into the mud, and they couldn't get it to turn. There were several other glitches, but they overcame them all. They moved the ship back and forth, as they had done with *Exodus* at its departure from Port Sète, and they finally left Burgas.

Ya'akov Salomon got the command of the twelve trains that set out on the journey. To execute the plan, he and his team concentrated immigration men in Europe, about thirty of them, as the trains left for Bulgaria, picking up refugees along the way at various collection points. They had to make sure the trains carrying more than fifteen thousand refugees crossed each border successfully (Russian, Hungarian, and so on) and reached the port of Burgas in Bulgaria in a sequence arranged beforehand, with an interval of four hours between each arrival.

The boarding procedure for the refugees onto the trains was complicated. Each train numbered thirty-five cars and three staff cars. The refugees boarded the first car, showed their legal tickets, got transferred to the second car for disinfection, and afterward were sent to the regular passenger cars. At every station refugees not included within this framework would sneak inside. The third car served as a detention car. Whoever wasn't listed was asked to get off at the next station. There was no choice, as they could jeopardize the entire undertaking.

In Giurgiu, on the border between Romania and Bulgaria, the Bulgarian authorities checked the documents of the passengers and permitted them to enter Bulgarian territory. At this point they had to take ferries across the Danube, which had already begun to freeze, to Ruse, where the Jews of the city welcomed them with cigarettes, apples, and wine. After a brief intermission they boarded the trains again—this time Bulgarian—and continued to Port Burgas.

Ultimately, 15,236 people arrived in twelve trains. The timetable was determined so that trains from the Russian and Hungarian borders would leave first, and four hours later the next train would depart. These were freight trains, at the height of winter. People stood linked together and freezing. In the closed cars they set up stoves, and people congregated around them. As it happened, a few people got burned, while those on the sides of the car remained frozen. Nevertheless, spirits were high.

Each train traveled for forty hours. En route, three children died. There was no time for a lengthy stop that would delay the journey, so the children were buried in the fields. Upon arrival in Burgas, the refugees received food and water rations for one day and were asked to relieve themselves in the immediate vicinity, because from the moment of their embarkation until departure they would have to remain in their places for a long time and would not have access to lavatories on the decks. The port city was a heap of ruins, and flocks of people wandered in search of a spot to relieve themselves, while taking turns to keep a lookout so as to forestall problems with the locals. Afterward, they marched according to prearranged sequences and boarded the ship. The final train was late owing to typical government red tape, drawn out by the Romanians to curry favor with the British. The process of embarking the refugees onto the ships lasted two consecutive days—forty-eight hours, by day and by night, in the bitter cold and in lashing rain. They formed military files and finally boarded the ships, on their way home at last. The British maintained their indefatigable efforts to enlist opposition by putting pressure on the Turks and the Romanians, but all this could not compete against the bribes that flowed this time in unusual abundance.

People were instructed to bring packages less than twenty kilograms each. Some brought chamber pots, coffeepots, and cups, and women dragged along washbasins and clothing. The crew tried delicately, firmly, compassionately, and angrily to persuade them that there was not enough room, and no other choice, but these people who were familiar with journeys from nowhere to nowhere no longer trusted anyone. With no other option, Yossi authorized orderlies by the gangplank to use their knives to cut any cargo that exceeded the allotted weight and let it fall into the water.

Yossi remembered the words of the British officer during the retreat from Greece, that it took ten months to build a ship, a month to make a tank, two days for a machine gun, half a day for a rifle, and for bullets just a few minutes, but it took eighteen years to make a soldier. Thus he told them, "You are more important than your things. You are leaving your clothes here, your belongings, and unnecessary personal stuff. When we arrive safely, you'll get everything from the agency."

On the steps there was chaos, and people tried to rescue their property, weeping and begging, but Yossi stood his ground. In his heart he knew that it was better they weep over their belongings, rather than have several hundred people be left behind for lack of space and weep over their bitter fate.

In case they were forced to clash with the British, as Yossi explained during his time with Shaul, they set up four derricks along the length of the ship and attached ropes to each of them so they could pull them all simultaneously onto the approaching ships. His Majesty's British fleet numbered at that time forty-five ships in a formation known as the Palestine Patrol, but Yossi calculated that not all of them would engage concurrently, as some were stationed at a considerable distance. In addition to the ships, the British activated seven armed speedboats and a division of the Royal Air Force from Palestine, Cyprus, Egypt, and Malta.

At the last moment a young rabbi showed up who tried to prevent the embarkation once the Sabbath started, and a brouhaha broke out. Finally another rabbi was found who said that according to Jewish law, if one Jew boarded before the Sabbath began, all the rest could board, and the uproar was forgotten. Even so, near the end of the embarkation, an additional delay developed when Yossi learned that a one-day-old baby died in the arms of its mother as she was on her way up the gangplank. She sobbed bitterly. The ushers, their patience tried, urged her to come aboard, but the mother refused to part from her dead chick. With heavy heart, Yossi decided to delay the departure further. He contacted a local rabbi, located a small wooden coffin, took the child for burial, and immediately afterward escorted the weeping mother back to the ship.

Sheyke Dan arrived by special plane from Sofia. At the eleventh hour he managed to prevent the deportation of five hundred boys, members of youth movements in Bulgaria, who, he promised the Bulgarian authorities, would depart on the *Pans*. Yossi knew that it was impossible to argue with Sheyke, so literally at the last moment another five hundred refugees from Bulgaria were added, thereby reducing the living quarters for each passenger to 47½ centimeters each. They had to lodge people on deck, despite the extreme cold. Yossi's only demand was that the process of their embarkation not take longer than twelve hours, because the refugees crammed in the ship's hold were in agony and had no more patience left.

The lost time had critical significance, because in the history of Aliyah Beth they had never planned such a colossal voyage, which hinged entirely on one crucial detail—the precise timing of passage through the Bosporus. Facing considerable delay in the timetable, and since the hour of passage was not amenable to change, Yossi decided that he had no other choice but to depart at night. According to the schedule, they had to reach the Bosporus with both ships no later than Sabbath midday.

The night weighed heavily on Yossi. He entered the floating cemetery of the Jewish people, bringing along with him 15,236 souls. More than anyone else, he knew the risk and the responsibility he bore.

Chapter Twenty-five

The *Pan York* and the *Pan Crescent* departed on Friday, December 26, 1947, at four in the afternoon, one after the other. Everybody came on deck; a crowd the equivalent of two cities in Palestine stood and sang "Hatikva." Yossi, who in his boyhood in Jerusalem heard his neighborhood friends singing "Hatikva" in secret, was deeply moved. Never before was this song, which became a national anthem, sung like this. Those who were there say the birds stopped flying and the wind ceased. The sea froze and stood still. Even the clouds didn't move. They said many things; whether or not it is true is far less important than the fact that they felt it was.

The people who had wandered on the roads, the trains, the passes, endured the endless embarkations, unloaded everything that was in their hearts against a Europe that was slowly fading in the distance; against the misery and humiliation that accompanied them everywhere, they lifted their eyes to the sweet, though frightening, unknown. Yossi stood among them, shaken. Young men, still in their twenties, taught to hold back all tears, were bringing the Jewish people to their homeland. It did not seem possible that in all the generations Jews had ever sung like this in such great numbers; it seemed now, though, that all the generations were together here for this one song.

The departure from Burgas southward toward Turkey would have shortened the voyage, but that route swarmed with uncharted minefields. The only route they could sail was northward, hugging the coast, along the territorial waters of Romania, where the minefields had been cleared by the Russians. It was a route that only the Russian navigators knew.

A pelting rain began after they set sail, and on the decks tarpaulin sheets were distributed for the refugees to wrap themselves in. Already at departure, Yossi was faced with the problem of choosing the course. He studied the timetables and realized that the powerful east wind could shift the mines into the route they were taking. He knew that traveling on this route at night was an awful gamble. And he knew that the Russian pilot who *had* the maps refused to sail at night. Yet there was no other option. Yossi understood the pilot, who, after all, had not taken this voyage as a Zionist. From the moment he learned that the voyage would take place at night, the ardent Communist never stopped crossing himself. He asked to be released from his job. Yossi decided to let him disembark at Varna along with Sheyke Dan and the Bulgarian officer who accompanied him. Out of gratitude, the pilot agreed to leave Yossi a copy of the map of the minefield. Yossi consulted with Gad Hilb, who was serving as captain, and together they tried to determine whether it was possible to cross this lethal sea with these maps, on their own. A scrupulous examination yielded a positive answer. At Varna they parted from Sheyke, the Bulgarian officer, and the Russian pilot. The *Pan York* departed first, with the *Pan Crescent* in its wake. Except for the pilot's map, they had no other protection against the mines. And as if the mines weren't enough of a danger, in the night they could barely make out the correct shoreline that was outlined by the buoys. It was December 27, 1947. Yossi and Gad Hilb stood on the pilot bridge in the longest night of their lives. It was cold, and a strong wind was blowing. The waves rose and crashed on the deck, and a raging foam covered the window in the room on the bridge. Each second stretched into an eternity of tiny fractions. They obsessively examined the compass and surveyed the maps.

They posted about thirty sharp-eyed youngsters to stand on the bow and lie at the sides of the *Pan York,* as Yossi had done on the road to Tel Mond when in charge of the mine-sweeping detail. They all focused their eyes on the water while the waves rose toward them and the wind threatened to blow them away, and they looked for floating mines. Such a mine, with half a ton of explosives in it, could take to the depths 7,500 human beings and severely injure the 7,500 others sailing in the rear on the *Pan Crescent*. In order to lower the probability of a double disaster, Yossi had ordered the *Pan Crescent* to follow in the wake of the *Pan York* and not deviate from its path.

In a furious downpour of rain, twenty-eight-year-old Yossi Harel had to make sure that he could continue to sail without endangering all the people aboard and that the thirty boys lying stretched on the bow and the sides of the ship would be able to spot an elusive object in the raging, murky sea. The boys changed shifts every few hours, using their eyes like field glasses, while the ship's searchlights shined over the bow and either side of the ship.

Yossi went through the roughest night of his life. If he made just one mistake, if one tiny, dark spot slipped from the sight of the boys or from his own sight, a disaster would have occurred. Every second he had to know precisely the height of the waves and the exact position of the ship. If one of the searchlights failed, the number of dead would have exceeded the number of residents of Rehovot and Rishon Le-Zion at that time, combined.

At a certain moment, the visibility declined owing to the tossing of the ship, and the mechanics were asked to work to their maximum capacity, aided by searchlights that barely pierced the menacing curtain of the night. It was a nightmare infused with a sense of mission. All eyes were riveted. A tense silence prevailed. On a sea in which 2,400 Jews had sunk to the bottom, Yossi Harel from Jerusalem led a convoy of more than 15,000 people. He reminded himself: "You are sailing a dark, cruel, cunning sea. You are advancing without knowing what awaits you a meter ahead. You must succeed."

With his next thought, his heart sank. How could one save thousands of people with fifty life belts? How could one protect the survivors of the Jewish people?

The crack of dawn appeared, and in the distance loomed the Romanian lighthouse marking the end of the zone of the route of death. A general sigh of relief was heard. Now it was possible to smile. Yossi stretched and went down to drink some tea. Although it seemed to everyone that an eternity had passed since they entered the channel, they made the passage in reasonable time and the zero hour was preserved. People began to come on deck in turns. Gad nodded at the wheel, completely relaxed.

For a brief while Yossi was tempted to feel at ease. But like the others, he knew that the real tests were yet ahead: Bosporus, Dardanelles, and His Majesty's fleet thirsty for revenge.

At the Romanian lighthouse they turned east and, at the speed of ten knots, sailed the territorial waters, then turned south. Midday Saturday they reached the Bosporus. Now all that remained was to see if the plan would work in the face of the myriad factors conspiring against them and against the enterprise. If it failed, all was for naught, and Bevin would be the victor.

The zero hour had been set two weeks earlier, at which time Moysh Perlman had met the Turkish commander of the Straits, who told him that the British were pressuring them to detain the ships for any mishap whatsoever. This, in spite of the existence of the international law that clearly prohibited the detention of ships in the Straits. Nevertheless, added the Turkish commander, it was always possible to use the pretext—as happened more than once—of deficient hygiene: every ship had to be inspected, and during inspection it was always possible to find some irregularity, detain the ship, summon the army, and then the British navy could swing into action.

It was clear they had to reach the Bosporus no later than midday Saturday, while the Turkish commander was on duty.

As they entered the Straits on Saturday, a group of Turkish officers and policemen boarded the *Pan York*. They looked serious, and the officer in charge announced: "If I don't sign, you don't pass."

Yossi told him he understood, handed him a gold-plated pen, and added: "Here, sign. It's worth signing with a proper pen, which is actually yours."

The officer looked at the pen somewhat hesitantly and asked: "And what about my comrades?"

And Yossi said: "They'll also sign with their own pens; here they are." Then Yossi asked: "Does the gentleman know what time it is now?" As the officer glanced at his watch, Yossi said: "How can a distinguished officer like you wear a watch like that!" And he handed him and his colleagues gold watches. Adding gold sovereigns, he said: "That takes care of both ships, eh?"

And the officer said: "Absolutely."

They disembarked, and the ships sailed securely across the Straits of the Bosporus, with clusters of people hanging like grapes from the decks, enjoying the landscape that passed slowly before their eyes. They reached Istanbul, the dock with all the large coffeehouses, where another pilot joined them. The British were content—after all, they were certain that the sanitation officers would detain the ship in accord with the agreed-upon procedure, claim something was amiss, then telephone the consul, and everything would get elegantly solved to their satisfaction and without their involvement.

What the British did not know was that by prior arrangement with Moysh Perlman, the Turkish commander would suddenly have to exit the city and leave just a minor official in the office. When the English would discover that the ships had proceeded beyond the sanitation inspection, the British commander would fume, telephone the Turk, and demand that he stop them immediately. But since it would be Saturday, the official would tell him that the commander was on holiday and would return only on Monday morning. The Turk would say, "Leave me your name, and when the general comes back, he'll contact you." And at the sixth call he would say, "Just give me a minute to write down the number."

So Yossi knew already in Burgas that they had to cross the marble sea and the Dardanelles no later than Sunday after midnight, because the general would have to return to his office before first light on Monday. When the ships passed Istanbul, Moysh Perlman was sitting near the waterfront in order to watch them go by. Alongside him stood three officials from the British embassy. He knew them. They stood with their backs to the water, gloating, "This time we stuck it to them!"

Because the voyage of the *Pans* was briefer than the others, there wasn't the same cultural activity as on the *Knesset Israel* and the *Exodus*. The children found a way to play games, some disputes arose over food, but with thousands of people under such conditions, it was impossible to dream of anything more orderly. Yossi was glad that the preparations had been so scrupulous; because the ships were large by the standards of Aliyah Beth, most of the refugees did not experience the disaster their predecessors had endured.

A Bulgarian girl who found favor in the eyes of a Romanian boy conducted a romance, mediated by one of the Spanish crew members who knew French. The Romanian spoke French and understood the girl's Ladino. There was always somebody there to translate their feelings and love. And during midday they held a concert with the classical records they took along with them everywhere. They kissed, and everyone who stood there clapped hands.

Problems over kosher food erupted immediately upon departure. The rabbis demanded that cooking on the Sabbath stop. Yossi and Berchik rejected the request out of hand. Then the rabbis came and demanded a ritual *mikveh*, in case any marriages should occur aboard ship. This time Yossi told them that by the laws of the sea, a captain could conduct a marriage ceremony in the presence of witnesses without any rabbis, and the hint was taken at once. In the end, one of the rabbis even participated in a marriage. He said the blessings and sang the seven benedictions. In this context a meeting of the crew was held, and one of the rabbis was assigned to publicize the legal decision that for preservation of life it was permitted to eat cooked food on the Sabbath. Lighting of Sabbath candles aboard ship was absolutely forbidden for reasons of safety, but the rabbis agreed that instead of a traditional candle-lighting ceremony, a few women from every compartment would say the blessings for everyone.

And there were those aboard ship who wanted to "look out for their friends." They were promptly informed that the distribution of water, food, and also the maintenance of order would be administered according to specifications and not according to the needs of one person or another. It was explicitly stated that the ship commander's authority overrode everything: We are at sea, and at sea the commander is supreme judge.

A secretariat was established including members of all the parties. Newspapers appeared in Romanian and Yiddish—matters concerning the Haganah appeared in Hebrew. If a child got lost, he would submit his number and orderlies would look after him. When it became known that a few anti-Ben-Gurion revisionists were armed, a curfew was announced and reliable orderlies were sent to comb every corner. Nothing was found. Apparently Yossi's quick and decisive response made an impact, and the weapons had been tossed into the sea.

At midnight they reached the Dardanelles. After the navigators disembarked, they sailed into the Aegean, which is the northern part of the Mediterranean Sea. Yossi could finally exhale. Here, the battle was over. The British wanted to prevent the ships from entering the Mediterranean Sea, but they were already there.

At first light, however, the bitter truth emerged: In serene confidence, a polished British fleet of ten warships lay in ambush.

Chapter Twenty-six

Yossi had never seen so many warships together. When the *Knesset Israel* came, three were waiting for it. When he brought the *Exodus*, six. Here were ten warships, like an honor escort or a hardened foe. But at this point it was obvious to everyone—the British and Yossi—that it was no longer possible to send them back to the Black Sea.

The British did not waste time. From the moment the fleet showed up, it was already in battle formation. They arrived flexing their muscles. Yossi gave considerable thought to what he was forbidden to do.

The crews on both ships went on alert, each person at his position. The news poured below deck, where heated arguments broke out. In contrast with the youngsters, who were eager for battle, the older ones who left Hungary, who had suffered and emerged from among the dead, were less joyous.

Yossi's sticking point was that the refugees not become cannon fodder now that the sea was a battlefield. "I can only send myself to kill or get killed. Not them." More than once he said: "I never cooperated in the sinking of *Exodus*, even in the most difficult moments, even when people were all for it. Kibbutz children aren't required to fight against the British, and do not die at the front. How much more so these children! I won't send them to die for the doubtful appearance of sanctification."

On one of the British ships, the *Ajax*, which Yossi remembered with bitterness from the *Exodus*, sat an admiral, the commander of the fleet in the eastern basin of the Mediterranean.

After the first circling, a tense stillness reigned. The British thought that the *Pan*s were armed with weapons and waited for them to take some step that might cause political damage to the Jews and allow them to teach the "Jewish bastards" once and for all a lesson they would not forget. They knew it was an enormous undertaking, and there wouldn't be many like it thereafter. They saw this as an excellent opportunity for payback to the obstinate Jews.

Nevertheless, a British soldier stationed on one of the ships described, years later, the frustration they felt as part of a gigantic fleet of modern ships chasing two tubs overflowing with babies and old people. And even if, by overtaking the ships, they had managed to beat and kill, and even if after the battle they had managed to collect some "made in America" food for their families in England—in such a fight there was no great honor.

Yossi brought these Jews to the Mediterranean because they had nowhere else to sail except in the direction of Palestine. With their own hands the British had destroyed some of the ovens in some of the camps. With their own eyes they had seen the piles of rotting bodies and the Germans who hastily buried thousands of Jewish corpses. They were among the liberators who had burned the barracks in rage and disgust and offered food to the survivors with compassion, pity, and loving-kindness. Nevertheless, here on the high seas, the British command made a strange and incomprehensible distinction with respect to those who remained alive.

After the *Exodus* and the indelible damage done to the British empire in the "enlightened world," the British were afraid to attack without a pretext. Yossi knew this and would certainly not provide them with one. He understood there was nothing the British wanted more than a small provocation. Based on the intelligence information they had in their hands, the British knew the Jews were ordered not to resist. They sought a way to break down the wall of common sense.

Yossi kept sailing toward Haifa. Unlike the British, he did not know that the die had already been cast. In an odd cable he received from Palestine, he was told that if the British turned to him, he should say that he had received instructions to follow their orders. He was astonished. Because the state was not yet fully established and power was not yet centralized, the cables in quick succession contradicted each other, and he was forced to resolve these contradictions as best he could. Until now, he had handled all the pressures on him from every side quite well, and he held on to his opinion that the struggle was over and victory imminent—the *Pan*s were on their way to Palestine.

In the next cable that he received was the order to inform the British that "God gave our father Abraham this land, and from this we are entitled to the land from our forefathers—therefore it is our land." Yossi was convinced that whoever had composed this cable had lost his mind. But the cable, it turned out later, had in fact been written by Ben-Gurion. Meanwhile, despite the presence of the British destroyers and cruisers, and despite the menacing British order to change direction and set sail toward Famagusta, the ships continued on their course to Haifa. The British, who sailed very close to them, spoke through a bullhorn and only later over the wireless. They insisted that their demands be met at once and threatened a bloodbath.

The cruiser *Mauritius*—the flagship of the British fleet— approached to within fifty meters of the *Pan York*. Yossi, Gad Hilb, and Nissan Livyatan stood on the pilot bridge and listened to the shouts of the soldiers waiting impatiently for the command to storm. They saw hundreds of fighters. They saw weapons aimed at them. The commander of *Mauritius* asked for the names of the ships.

This was a perplexing request. Because of conflicting opinions within the leadership, the ships had not yet been given Hebrew names. But the sea had its own laws, and at sea a ship had to identify itself by name. Yossi cabled Palestine, asking what to say. After a nerve-racking exchange of cables, he was informed that he should say that the names of the ships were *The Friend* and *The Sister*. There was a mix-up in the instructions, and the cables for *The Friend* reached *The Sister* and vice versa. The names, though, remained neutral.

Then Yossi decided to return to the original names, *Pan York* and *Pan Crescent*. Again scores of cables were exchanged. Each leader felt that he should express an opinion. Meanwhile the British admiral received far more complicated particulars, such as the number of women and children on the ships, but not the ships' names. Only near midday did a compromise arrive from Palestine: *The Ingathering* and *Independence*.

Yossi was disappointed that the Haganah's name was missing, as had been the case with the *Knesset Israel* and the *Exodus*, but he was told this was the final authoritative decision. The admiral turned now to Yossi, asking him to discontinue any provocations and sail in the direction of Famagusta. It pained Yossi that the greatest undertaking in the history of illegal immigration, which had involved so much preparation, would remain without even an appropriate name. After he returned to the clichés formulated in Ben-Gurion's cables concerning the promise given to Abraham on behalf of the Jews and the matter of the promised land, he declared: "Since there are no weapons on the ship, the British are permitted to come aboard on the following conditions—they won't conduct any searches, they won't come armed, and the crew will be treated just like the refugees."

The English listened, passed on the information, and waited for a reply. They were disappointed when they realized that a battle would not take place here, particularly because it meant that they could not arrest the crew members. But the admiral actually felt better when it was clear that the matter was coming to a close. After a sharp telegraphic dispute, the commander told Yossi that he accepted the conditions in full and asked him to stop the ships. Likewise he reported that he would bring crew members of his own onto the *Pan York* and the *Pan Crescent*.

Yossi replied that he agreed, but "I won't stop until I receive an unambiguous answer concerning the crew members." He also added that if he didn't get an answer quickly, he would sail again directly for Haifa, and the responsibility for the bitter consequences of the ensuing battle would fall solely on the admiral. He concluded by saying: "The crew members remain with the refugees, the command of both ships will transfer to the British, but the communications equipment will stay in the hands of the crew. All the belongings will remain with the refugees," and again he emphasized in forceful fashion, "There will be no distinction between crew and refugees."

Yossi knew that even if he were to be arrested, his prospects were excellent compared with those of the Spanish crew, who would be deported to their country of origin, so he fought vigorously on behalf of these Spaniards. The admiral didn't understand. What was up with this man? What did he really want? Why was he so obstinate? Time passed; it was a hard decision, explicit instructions never arrived from headquarters, neither from Cairo nor from London. But Yossi kept up the pressure. Either these conditions got accepted or he would sail to Haifa.

Chapter Twenty-seven

The British understood that at this historic moment the bringing of 15,236 Jews could be construed in the eyes of the Arabs as the introduction of 15,236 fighters, and that would be taken badly. A naval battle now would be a dead loss. Even if they won, it would be to their shame and discredit in the eyes of the whole world—for even if the rest of the world wasn't at all interested in the fate of the Jews, its conception of justice hinged on the notion that good guys are always outnumbered but ultimately prevail.

After the refugees on the *Exodus* were returned to Germany, there were people who began paying attention to what was happening in Palestine. Finally there were people who leveled criticism against the British empire, against its deliberations and deeds in the Near East.

After three hours the admiral's answer came: He accepted all conditions, including the clause on the crew. The admiral would take upon himself the responsibility vis-à-vis his superiors. He gave Yossi his word of honor he would not search for the crew or harm them. Yossi accepted his pledge. The British admiral asked in amazement whether he accepted this without written confirmation, and Yossi answered: "A British admiral's word of honor is stronger than any written confirmation." Now, even if the admiral had planned some scheme, it was already too late.

Thus it was established that at two in the afternoon the British would board the ships, and not the Jews but the British would bring the refugees to Famagusta, so that the Arabs wouldn't see

15,236 Jews entering Palestine. Some of the refugees aboard ship wanted to fight, and to the objections against submission that were hurled at him, Yossi replied that he was following the orders he had received. His hidden daredevil self also hated to surrender and wanted to strike back at the scoundrels for how they had treated the *Exodus*. But sober judgment concluded otherwise. He knew that he must not succumb to his emotions and that victory didn't necessarily derive from who killed whom, especially in a battle doomed from the start.

The ships now stood with their prows against the wind, and the British officers and sailors who boarded the decks were unarmed and, in keeping with Yossi's request, also without helmets. Boarding the bridge and taking over the command, they looked scared as hundreds of eyes flashing with hatred stared at them. They did not realize that the young man standing alongside them, called Amnon, was the actual commander of the "Jewish pirate" ships.

It was an uncommon drama that brought neither honor nor glory to either side. Yossi was now vulnerable. Conflicting cables had come from the various headquarters of the Jewish organizations. Some people complained. Yossi saw the group of Hungarian women whose eyes pleaded to bring them to any destination whatsoever. The women had met each other during the long journey by train and bonded together. Each of them had lost a brother, or husband, or children. To Yossi they looked like mourners in a Greek tragedy, the chorus bearing the decree of *moira*—fate.

The expression on their faces encouraged and supported the young man who knew, on the one hand, that he had to fight because in keeping with Greek tragedy he was a hero, but who on the other hand also knew, with equal certainty, that he had to concede in order not to convert these women into fighters on the Palestinian front.

Through negotiations with the English, they tried to determine what would be the fate of the ships after disembarkment and exactly how the disembarkment would be carried out. The Spaniards managed to mingle with the refugees, and all the details were already adjusted. It was the last night.

The British stood on the pilot's bridge, and Yossi went looking for the Spaniards. They were at the stern, in a place where the British could not see them. He made a going-away party for them. They drank wine. Yossi related how in his youth he wanted to join the fight for the Republic. The Spaniards knew that it was on their account the negotiations had taken so long. They knew there had been but one step between them and death. They were somewhat intoxicated and exhausted. They sang the song of the Fifth Brigade and recited poems by García Lorca and Pablo Neruda, poems Yossi remembered well from his youth. The atmosphere was one of warmth and nostalgia. Yossi promised he would be sure to employ them in future.

At the close of the little celebration, a man in his early thirties came by and stopped. When he heard the song of the Fifth Brigade, he began to cry. Steve, a Spaniard, looked at him and invited him to join them. The man was flustered but sat down.

Steve gave him a piercing look and said: "It seems that something connected to Spain says something to you."

The man said: "My name is Joseph, and I had a brother who died there." Steve asked for his brother's name. Joseph said: "Yehudah."

Now Steve looked flustered, too, and said: "I knew him. He was a gem, everyone loved him. He could recite in five languages, and at night we would listen to his declamations. He had a soft voice and lovely eyes, blue eyes, like yours. He was short, thin, blond haired." Steve hushed for a moment, then added: "He was killed not far from me, after I fled from the port."

For a moment Joseph appeared to smile and said: "That's strange, someone else asked me about my brother—that's actually the reason why I'm alive."

Joseph drank and told how he and his brother came to Palestine in 1932. They were active Communists. The British deported them in 1937. "My brother," said Joseph, "traveled to Paris, and from there went to fight in Spain. I traveled to the city where we were born in Poland, because we still had brothers there. The city was near the German border. When war broke out, my older brother fled to Russia, because he thought he could make a contribution there, but as far as I know he was arrested and died in a Soviet detention camp. The Germans stayed in our town until 1943 and didn't take us to a camp. We heard what was happening, tried to escape, but our Polish neighbors 'protected us.' After all, we were fair game, a Jew was worth a loaf of bread or a few potatoes.

"In 1943, before the Germans left town, they sent all the Jews to Auschwitz. I had a sweetheart. Her name was Leah. She was already separated from me on the train. My parents went straight to death, and I worked as a painter. I was good at it, and I would recite, yes, like my brother, we're all orators in our family, our grandfather was the best preacher in town. I loved my girlfriend. She apparently died. I looked for her all over Europe and never found her.

"One day—and here I come to the business of my brother and Spain—a non-Jewish Kapo approached me, a German, and asked me if I had a brother. I thought, This is it, he's come to take me, and I said yes, I had a brother. He asked me if my brother's name was Yehudah. I said yes. And then the Kapo told me he was a Communist and knew my brother, together they fought in the International Brigade, and my brother was a darling, a joker, and a declaimer. He advised me to join the underground set up in the camp, and said they needed turpentine, which was in the storeroom where I got paint.

"I brought the material, and someone mixed it with other ingredients and concocted a bomb, and that's how we executed the famous sabotage of the gas installation. We weren't caught;

that is, neither I nor the German was caught. Others, yes. Where he is today, I don't know.

"After liberation, I wandered. I reached the British occupation zone and met some Palestine Jews from Bricha. I knew Hebrew because I had lived in Palestine, so I was able to help them. The British captured me and put me in prison with Nazis I knew from the German camp where they took me, in the death march, after they cleared out of Auschwitz. They spat and pissed on me, and the English stood by and laughed.

"And since then I continued to look for Leah, and I never found her. Then I learned she died. Now I am here. In the meantime I met a lovely woman, got married, my wife is pregnant, and I want to live as close as possible to Jerusalem."

Steve was deeply moved. The Spanish seamen continued to sing. Yossi had already returned to the pilot bridge. Perhaps things were coming full circle . . . Jerusalem.

In Cyprus, *Pan York* and *Pan Crescent* anchored by the pier. Yossi saw the English at the port, and they seemed ready for action.

Feverish deliberations were conducted over the wireless about how people could enter without registering their names, so as to protect the Spaniards. The English began to renege on their agreements. Apparently the admiral was fuming over his obligation to Yossi. Yossi would not give in. In the end his word of honor was upheld, and disembarkment proceeded as agreed. A British officer standing there indicated dryly that apart from the stench emanating from the Jewish ships, everything went peacefully.

The British admiral surrounded by soldiers, along with a brigadier of the Sixth Paratroopers Unit and other officers, asked who the commander was. Yossi introduced himself—a twenty-eight-year-old, a boy. The admiral refused to believe it. As they spoke, a girl approached, squeezed Yossi's hand, and stuck a note inside containing the contact code to the Haganah underground in the refugee camp. When he made contact, he learned that the British had arrested Gadda Shochet, one of those in charge of the fitting of the *Pan*s. They had chanced on the fact that he'd once served as a pilot in the Royal Air Force and therefore was defined as a deserter and arrested.

Yossi instructed the refugees to stop disembarking from the ships at once. People stopped. Pandemonium broke out. British officials scampered all around. He explained to the admiral that the arrest of Gadda Shochet violated the agreement between them. Gadda was one of his crew members. Gadda was released, and the refugees continued to disembark.

According to the permanent orders under which Yossi worked, his responsibility ended with the disembarkation from the ship. Stationed in Cyprus were Palmach men and commanders of ships captured earlier, and it was their task to handle everything there. Yossi left the camp through a tunnel dug from one of the tents beyond the fences. Somewhere near the seashore, a fishing boat from Palestine was supposed to be waiting for him and half a dozen other ship commanders, with equipment and identity papers for all of them.

The tunnel was narrow, and with great difficulty they managed to crawl through. Yossi reached the other side, where a Haganah man was waiting for him. He took him and the crew to two Greek underground vehicles that drove them to an agreed-upon hideaway, to await the fishing boat. They waited at night for three or four hours, but the boat did not show up. At first light, while still hidden among the rocks, they suddenly heard gunshots. They feared they were discovered but in the end learned that the shots were fired harmlessly by Cypriot hunters.

After about an hour they were joined by two others who informed them that the fishing boat *Eagle* was delayed and would arrive only tomorrow morning. And indeed, the next day they boarded it with the aid of rubber rafts. They sailed among the British warships swarming in the region. At first they sailed in the direction of Beirut and afterward turned south to Caesarea. There they all disembarked, except for Yossi.

He removed the refugee garments he wore, leather jacket, fur hat, and boots, and put on normal clothing upon arriving in Tel Aviv.

When he boarded bus #5 to ride home, he fished in his pocket and couldn't find any money. He turned to the driver and said in embarrassment that he forgot his money at home. The driver refused to let him stay on the bus.

This man of twenty-eight—a fighter for the rebirth of Israel—did not say a word. He got off the bus and, without any bitterness in his heart, walked home by foot.

Chapter Twenty-eight

In the morning, at the Tel Aviv beach, Yossi had thought definitively, We accomplished something. Nearly four hundred thousand refugees crossed the continent on their way to Eretz Israel. They walked to the coasts and waited until they could come. A portion of them made it. On the *Dalin*, the first ship sent by the Mossad le-Aliyah Beth at the end of the war in August 1945, there were 35 refugees. On the two *Pans*, which basically sealed the saga of illegal immigration, there were 15,236 refugees in all.

However, emptiness accompanied him on his way home. He felt like someone returning from the battlefield. He had brought two cities on the *Pans*. A war was raging, there were bloody clashes. He realized the circle had closed and that the rest of his life began from that moment on.

After *Exodus* came the War of Independence. The first chapter ended, and a new chapter began.

After the two *Pans*, Yossi set out on his way that lasted many more years, on missions mostly secret. And all these years he lived with the *Exodus*—the *Exodus* from Europe—as a motto, as a justification for existence, as a permit to believe in what seemed to him the path of justice.

After all, the *Exodus* did not come all by itself. Millions, dead and alive, accompanied it, dreamers accompanied it, a continuous struggle accompanied it. A child buried at sea accompanied it, tied to the chain of the anchor. A dark stain in the history of nations accompanied it. The doors shut in the faces of people who were never wanted accompanied it. A righteous non-Jew like

Raoul Wallenberg accompanied it, a man who saved Jews in Hungary and disappeared. Jews like Hillel Kook accompanied it, Jews who worked and managed to do the little that was possible to be done in the face of the indifference and cruelty of the Allies. The thunderous silence of the churches accompanied it, the silence of newspapers the world over, of the most high-minded men of the world, of British intellectuals who saw how their government was transporting refugees of the Holocaust back to Germany and kept silent. A woman who died in childbirth accompanied it. Three of its fatal casualties accompanied it, the young American volunteer Bill Bernstein, the twenty-three-year-old member of Hashomer Hatzair, Mordechai Boimstein, and the fifteen-year-old boy Zvi Yakobovitz from the Dror orphanage accompanied it.

Thousands of blue candles accompanied it, 200 wounded, 2,437 refugees who drowned in the floating cemeteries en route to Palestine, which they never reached. The 700 unfortunate refugees of Kladovo accompanied it, refugees who were taken to the Danube and got stuck in its frozen waters and then were made to run naked in the cold and dig a huge pit for themselves, where they were shot. The sunken *Struma*, *Mefkure*, and *Salvador* accompanied it. In all, 115,000 Jewish refugees who succeeded against all the odds accompanied it.

They were the sacrifices, they were the scarred refugees, and they are the Jewish state.

Glossary

Balfour Declaration: Official statement in the form of a letter to Baron Rothschild from foreign minister Balfour, then the head of the Zionist Federation of England, dated November 2, 1917, expressing support "for the establishment of a Jewish National Home in Palestine." The British government pledged to "use their best endeavors to facilitate the achievement of this object." (Most historians concur that the British declaration was aimed at furthering British military and strategic interests in the area.)

Bricha: Jewish group that helped refugees organize illegally in hostile territories. (Literal definition: flight)

British Mandate: In July 1922, Britain was awarded the Mandate for Palestine by the League of Nations to implement the principles of the Balfour Declaration through negotiations with "an appropriate Jewish Agency . . . by facilitating Jewish immigration . . . and encouraging close settlement on the land." The Mandate came to an end on May 17, 1948, when the United Nations voted in favor of Israel's sovereignty.

CID: Criminal Investigation Department of the British police in the colonies.

FOSH: Field units led by Yitzhak Sadeh, made up of members of the former Nomads contingent.

Haganah: Official Jewish underground army during the British Mandate. Established in 1920 and went on until 1948, at which point it served as the basis for the Israeli Army.

Halutz: Literally, a pioneer. Refers to a Zionist youth movement that started in Eastern Europe in 1900 and lasted only a few years after the State of Israel was founded in 1948.

Hanita: First Jewish settlement in Palestine under the white paper, located in the upper Galilee near Lebanon. Founded in 1938 at the height of the Arab riots with the aim of gaining a foothold in a region that was until then utterly devoid of Jewish settlement.

"Hatikva": Song written by Naftali Hertz Imber that became Israel's National Anthem.

Irgun: Extreme right-wing underground Jewish organization that was not under *yishuv* orders. Founded in 1937, the Irgun fought the Arabs until 1939, when it aimed its attacks on the British.

Joint Distribution Committee: American Jewish committee established in 1941 that set out to provide aid to refugees from Europe.

Masada: Herod's royal citadel and the last outpost of the Zealots during the Jewish War against Rome (66–70/73) that has served as a symbol for martyred Jews ever since; situated on top of an isolated rock on the edge of the Judean Desert and the Dead Sea Valley.

Mossad le-Aliyah Beth: Organization for Illegal Immigration, established in 1934 by Jews in Palestine to facilitate the transport of refugees wanting to leave an increasingly hostile Europe for Palestine, but unable to do so by legal means.

Palmach: Permanently mobilized militant leg of the Haganah that was established in 1941; now refers to the national and regional fighting reserve of the Israeli Army.

Sabra: Israeli-born Jew.

TTG: Sham British unit comprised of members of the Mossad who were better able to expedite underground missions in Europe in the guise of British soldiers. (TTG is an abbreviation for *Tilches Tizi Geschaeft,* derived from the Arabic *Tilches Tizi,* meaning "kiss my ass," and the German *Geschaeft*, meaning "business" i.e. monkey business.)

White Paper: Official British government policy statement issued on May 17, 1939 that severely curtailed legal immigration to Palestine. This coincided with the fierce rise in German persecution of the Jews in Europe that rendered the Jews' need for a place of refuge desperate. In 1940 only 10,643 Jews were allowed to enter; in 1941 only 4,592; in 1942 only 4,206.

UNSCOP: United Nations Special Committee on Palestine appointed by the UN General Assembly in May 1947; an Anglo-American committee set up to investigate the Arab-Israeli conflict and recommend whether British involvement should continue.

Yishuv: General name for the Jewish community in Palestine before the establishment of the State of Israel.

Zionist Congress: International parliament established by Theodor Herzl in the 1890s that convened for the first time in Basel, Switzerland. Herzl's aim was "to close the Zionist ranks, bring about an understanding between all Zionists and to unify their endeavors," and to establish "the national assembly of the Jewish people."

List of Sources

Books and Articles in Hebrew:

Shaul Avigur, *Im Dor Hahaganah* (vol. 2). Tel Aviv: Ma'arakhot, Ministry of Defense, 1977. (*With the Generation of the Haganah*)

Reuven Aharoni, *Mutot Toren*. Ramat Efal: ha-Mercaz le-toldot ko'akh ha-magen ha-Haganah, al shem Yisra'el Gelili, 1997. (*Leaning Masts*)

Aryeh L. Avneri, *Mi-Velos ad Ta'urus*. Tel Aviv: Yad Tabenkin/ ha-Kibbutz ha-me'ukhad, 1986. (*From Velos to Taurus*)

Michael Alder, *Anshoi haTselalim—TTG*. Tel Aviv: Ministry of Defense, 1997. (*Shadow Men*)

Yehuda Bauer, *Diplomatya u-makhteret ba-mediniyut ha-tsiyonit 1939–1945*. Tel Aviv: Sifriyat ha-po'alim, 1963. (*From Diplomacy to Resistance: A History of Jewish Palestine, 1939-1945*)

Yehuda Bauer, *Ha-Brikha*. Tel Aviv: Moreshet, Sifriyat ha-po'alim (undated). (*The Flight*, or *The Brikha Movement*)

Nahum Bogner, *Sphinot ha-meri, ha-ha'pala*, 1945–1948. Tel Aviv: Ministry of Defense, 1993. (*Ships of Revolt, the Illegal Immigration*)

Isaiah Berlin, *Al Yitzhak Sadeh*. Tel Aviv: Davar, 1986. (*On Yitzhak Sadeh*)

Zerubavel Gilad (ed.), *Sefer ha-Palmach*. Tel Aviv: ha-Kibbutz ha-me'ukhad, 1953. (*The Book of the Palmach*)

Shaul Dagan, *ha-Fosh*. Tel Aviv: Ministry of Defense, 1995. (*Special Field Units of the Haganah*)

Shaul Dagan, *Tokhnit ha-tsafon*. Tel Aviv: Ministry of Defense, 1994. (*Carmel Plain*)

Tzvika Dror (ed.), *Be-ikvot dapei edut*. Bet lokhame ha-geta'ot: ha-Kibbutz ha-me'ukhad, 1984. (*Pages of Testimony*)

Ze'ev Hadari and Zev Tsakhor, *Oniyot o medinah, Korot oniyot ha-ma'pilim ha-gdolot "Pan York," u-"Pan Crescent."* Beersheba, undated. (*Ships or State, the Saga of the Large Illegal Immigration Ships*)

Hana Weiner and Dalia Ofer, *Parshat Kladovo Shabats, Masah ha-ha'palah shelo hushlam*. Tel Aviv: Am oved, 1992. (*Dead-End Journey: The Tragic Story of the Kladavo Sabac Group*)

Avraham Zohar, *ha-Komando ha-yami ba-Palmach*. Tel Aviv: Tag, 1994. (*The Naval Commando of the Palmach*)

Idit Zartel, *Zehavam shel ha-Yehudim*. Tel Aviv: Am Oved, 1996. (*Gold of the Jews, or From Catastrophe to Power*)

Amnon Yonah, *Le-lo akevot*. Tel Aviv: Ma'arakhot, 1965. (*Without Footprints*)

Christopher Seiks, *Orde Wingate*. Tel Aviv: Ma'arakhot, 1951.

Yehuda Slutsky (ed.), *Sefer toldot ha-Haganah* (vols. 2–3). Tel Aviv: Ma'arakhot, Am Oved, 1972. (*The History of the Haganah*)

Dalia Ofer, *Derekh ba-yam: Aliyah bet bi-tekufat ha-Shoah*. Jerusalem: Yad Ben-Zvi, 1988. (*By Way of the Sea: Aliyah Beth During the Period of the Holocaust*)

Avraham Fuchs, *Karati ve-en oneh*. Jerusalem: Private publication, 1984. (*The Unheeded Cry*)

Gershon Rivlin (ed.), *Ale-zayit ve-kherev*. Tel Aviv: Ministry of Defense, 1990. (*Olive Leaves and Sword*)

Mordechai Russell, *Tik Mafkorah*. Tel Aviv: ha-Va'adah le-pe'ulot rukhaniypt Yehudei Romania, 1981. (*The Mafkorah File*)

Anita Shapira, *Yehudim khadashim, Yehudim yeshanim*. Tel Aviv: Am Oved, 1997. (*New Jews, Old Jews*)

Gabi Sarig, *haGid'onim*. Ramat Efal: ha-Mercaz le-toldot ko'akh ha-magen ha-Haganah al shem Yisra'el Gelili, 1988. (*The Wireless Operators*)

Sources in English:

Auschwitz: Beginning of a New Era? New York: Ktav Publishing House, The Cathedral Church of St. John the Divine, 1977.

Ruth Altbeker Cypris, *A Jump for Life*. London: Constable, 1997.

Lucy Davidowicz, *The War Against the Jews, 1933–1945*. New York: Holt, Rinehart and Winston, 1975.

Leonard Gross, *The Last Jews of Berlin*. London: Sidgwick & Jackson, 1983.

Aviva Halamilsh, *The Exodus Affair: Holocaust Survivors and the Struggle for Palestine*. New York: Syracuse University Press, 1998.

Ewa Kurek, *Your Life is Worth Mine*. New York: Hippocrene Books, 1997.

The Diary of David Sierakowiak. London: Bloomsbury, 1996.

Leon Poliakov, *Harvest of Hate*. Syracuse, NY: Syracuse University Press, 1954.

Sol Stern, *Roosevelt and the Jews, The Village Voice* (undated).

David S. Wyman, *The Abandonment of the Jews: America and the Holocaust, 1941–1945*. New York: Pantheon, 1984.

Secondary Sources:

The Archives for the History of the Haganah in memory of Eliyahu Golumb.

The personal documents of Yitzhak Sadeh.

Tik Palyam (Ha-Pluga Ha-Yamit): Files of the Palmach's Naval Corps.

Logs of the following ships: *Exodus, Knesset Israel, Nisnit.*

The British Admiralty Orders, 1947.

Documentary Films:

Exodus '47.

America and the Holocaust, PBS American Experience Series, 1994.

Haim Gouri, The Last Sea, Kibbutz Lochamei Hagetaot.

Andrea Hoffman, Exodus Kinder, Hamburg: Filmproduktion, 1997.